Calgary Papers
in Military and Strategic Studies

Editor

Dr. John Ferris

Guest Editors

Lara Olson
and Dr. Hrach Gregorian

Production Editor: JoAnn Cleaver
Cover: Vangool Design

Cover photo used with permission of the
International Security Assistance Force (ISAF) – NATO
Canadian Cataloguing in Publication Data:
Printed and Bound in Canada
ISBN # 978-0-88953-329-5

Centre for Military and Strategic Studies
MacKimmie Library Tower 701
University of Calgary
2500 University Drive NW
Calgary, AB T2N 1N4
Tel: 403.220.4030 / Fax: 403.282.0594
www.cmss.ucalgary.ca / cmsspub@ucalgary.ca

Centre for Military and Strategic Studies

Calgary Papers
in Military and Strategic Studies

Civil-Military Coordination: Challenges and Opportunities in Afghanistan and Beyond; Vol. 3, 2008

Series Editor: Dr. John Ferris

Guest Editors:
Lara Olson and Dr. Hrach Gregorian

Table of Contents

Articles

Civil-Military Coordination: Challenges and Opportunities in Afghanistan and Beyond

Lara Olson and Hrach Gregorian, Co-Directors of PDSP, the Peacebuilding, Development and Security Program

Editorial Notes

The Peacebuilding, Development, and Security (PDS) Program was initiated at the University of Calgary in 2007 with funding from the University Centre for Military and Strategic Studies (CMSS). It represents a partnership between CMSS and the Institute of World Affairs (IWA), based in Arlington, Virginia. The papers republished here expand on presentations made at an expert workshop[1] – **Coordinated Approaches to Security, Development, and Peacekeeping: Lessons Learned from Afghanistan and Liberia*** – held in Calgary in March of 2007 by these two organizations.

The workshop brought together thirty-five expert practitioners from international assistance agencies, donors, military forces active in Afghanistan and Liberia, along with representatives of the national government and national NGOs to review lessons learned from ongoing international peace operations in the two countries. The aim was to better understand the gap between the policy-level consensus promoting greater aid coordination and coherence in recent years and the actual practice in the field. This issue is significant but little examined, perhaps because it lies at the intersection between traditional conceptions of defence policy, peacekeeping, and the work of NGOs.

The *Journal of Military and Strategic Studies* first published the articles generated from that conference on-line as a topic in its own right under the auspices of the journal's co-editors, ***John Ferris*** and ***James Keeley.***

Calgary Papers in Military and Strategic Studies is pleased to feature these materials in its final issue of 2008.

---

* for detailed workshop reports and a policy brief synthesizing recommendations for practice from this research effort, see <http://www.ucalgary.ca/pdsp/node/34>.

GUEST EDITORS' INTRODUCTION

To the layperson, the term "civil-military coordination" evokes notions of a seamless division of labour between aid workers and international military forces. Media coverage of crises areas like Somalia, Bosnia, Kosovo, Sierra Leone, and Afghanistan reinforces this expectation, showing relief agencies distributing food and medicines under the guard of heavily armed soldiers, or aid workers and military personnel working together to construct refugee camps, set up field hospitals, provide emergency water and sanitation, etc. Publics of donor countries like Canada that provide relief and development aid as well as troops to such missions expect efficient teamwork as a matter of course, and donor governments and the United Nations have adopted many policies advocating closer integration of the various assistance streams known variously as "3D" (defence, development, and diplomacy) or "whole-of-government" approaches, or within the UN, as "integrated missions".

The problem is that this image of civil-military teamwork is too simplistic and it assumes too much. The prevailing approach frames coordination as a technical exercise that the right combination of meetings, information flow, and coordination focal points can solve. It also frames civil-military coordination as an accepted goal. Yet in areas of active conflict and in fragile, post-conflict settings, the mandates, timeframes, guiding principles, and methodologies for how civilian aid agencies and military forces work are radically different and they often clash, despite good intentions and a sincere common desire to "help the people" shared by most international military and civilian aid personnel involved in international peace operations.

The focus of the March workshop was much broader than civil-military coordination; its goal was to analyze the broad dynamics of mission-wide coordination amongst the enormous array of governmental, intergovernmental, and non-governmental actors that comprise these complex international missions for peace. However, many insights on civil-military relationships in the field emerged, and the authors discussed here, all participants in that workshop, agreed to develop their presentations further into the articles included in this special issue. These contributions present very different viewpoints on the most effective relationship between civilian and military assistance providers, but all agree that authentic, common strategies amongst such unlike international assistance actors are not emerging from current civil-military coordination approaches, which too often focus on field-level interactions, civil-military liaison, and mechanistic structures of integration. A detailed outline of each follows this brief overview.

Stapleton claims that current civil-military coordination models have not helped achieve security and development goals better or faster in Afghanistan. Capstick's contribution to this issue strongly supports current models of civil-military coordination and integration, but cautions that they do not go far enough, nor do they reflect a sincere, strategic-level alignment between security and development agendas in Afghanistan. Cornish documents the inherent difficulties and challenges, as well as the trade-offs made for the protection of civilians and their right to assistance, that are posed by such integrated approaches. De Coning's piece argues that the structures for civil-military coordination in UN integrated missions (often seen as a model) have deliberately limited goals and were never meant to harmonize the broader security/development agendas of the mission. Finally, our own contribution (Olson and Gregorian) argues that trade-offs between important values and goals held by these diverse international assistance actors have been masked behind blanket prescriptions for greater coherence and coordination, and that the lack of truly inclusive processes to deal with these fundamental differences undermines any sincerely common approach.

This collection unpacks these diverse orientations, and by bringing in views from the NGO sector, also questions the notion of a common "civilian" side of the civil-military equation. Civilian assistance encompasses entities as varied as donor government development agencies or political missions; the UN, the World Bank and other intergovernmental bodies, as well as the vast spectrum of non-governmental organizations (hereafter NGOs) and civil society organizations who, in some sectors, implement up to 90 per cent of internationally funded programs. In Afghanistan, many international and national NGOs, concerned to preserve their independence, neutrality, and operational space, resist greater integration with the more politically driven agendas of the UN and government donors and with international military forces. Consequently, civilian agencies can be more different than alike, and there is much disparity between government agencies with a clear need to get "their internal house in order" and those NGOs who may not see themselves as part of the "team" but who in fact do most of the work on the ground.

This issue delves into this debate to offer an opportunity to hear frank views from all quarters on the challenges and opportunities posed by civil-military coordination (in Afghanistan, in particular, but also more generally). Only with a more balanced view of both sides of the coin is it possible to devise effective strategies to meet the real needs of populations caught up in conflict for security, relief, development, and ultimately, for sustainable peace.

We thank the Centre for Military and Strategic Studies for the opportunity to profile these issues. The PDS Program is proud to present this collection from leading experts and highly experienced practitioners who know intimately the difficult dynamics of current civil-military coordination experiences in Afghanistan as well as from their work in many other crisis settings.

Barbara Stapleton's outlook is rooted in decades of international human rights work and in her experience in Afghanistan over the past six years, first as Advocacy and Policy Coordinator with the Agency Coordinating Body for Afghan Relief (ACBAR), the main NGO coordination body based in Kabul, and since May 2006, as a Deputy to the EU Special Representative for Afghanistan. She leads us through a detailed review of the evolution of the main mechanism for civil-military coordination in Afghanistan, the Provincial Reconstruction Teams (PRTs). She argues that while their impact on security and reconstruction has been disappointing, their main impact to date – that of sustaining international engagement – has been political in nature.

In her view, PRTs have kept donors engaged by responding more to the needs of the international community than to the needs of Afghans. Her review of the political, human, and organizational dynamics that have shaped PRTs over the last five years emphasizes the non-linear and ad hoc nature of their evolution, outlining how PRTs reflect a very disjointed, donor-driven, international engagement in Afghanistan that suffers from too many autonomous organizations in lead roles. She maintains that PRTs have effectively generated the appearance of progress, but that they have, in fact, been unable to address key political issues that undermine the whole effort in the provinces.

In support of her position, she contends primarily that PRTs got the focus wrong by addressing the security needs of the Afghan State instead of those of the Afghan people. This prompted Afghans to conclude that PRTS are largely irrelevant to their physical security. She believes the international community has overestimated the value of concrete reconstruction aid, and that a more consistent defense of the human security of the Afghan people would have better established the moral intent of the international presence in Afghanistan. Furthermore, the perceived "success" of the PRT concept in terms of expanding the numbers of PRTs and nations involved has resulted in a "Balkanization" of the aid effort that has, paradoxically, undermined the goals of state building. Ultimately she argues that the civil-military relationship and the PRT concept have absorbed too much energy and political will, and in fact, have diverted attention from the real issues threatening Afghanistan's recovery.

Colonel Mike Capstick (retired) brings a perspective grounded in thirty-two years of service with the Canadian Armed Forces and as the Commander of the first deployment of the Canadian Forces Strategic Advisory Team in Afghanistan – the mixed military-civilian team providing strategic planning advice and capacity building to the Afghan government. Capstick argues that civil-military coordination specifically, and coordination overall, are weak in the Afghan mission and that too often, civil-military coordination issues are discussed only at the tactical level, neglecting the more important strategic level. He faults the mission overall for both "strategic incoherence" and for an "economy of force" approach to both security and reconstruction assistance.

In his view, effective coordination in the Afghan mission at the strategic level means following the lead of the broad framework agreed upon by the international community and the Afghan government, the Afghanistan Compact, and its embedded framework for development, the Afghanistan National Development Strategy (ANDS). Guided by these frameworks, he argues that a "unity of effort" approach must be part of the operating culture of every single entity involved, civilian and military.

Reviewing the Canadian Forces' experience along with other departments of the Canadian government in security, development, and governance work, he contends that old distinctions between civilian and military roles are no longer relevant in Afghanistan. Furthermore, he notes that contexts like Afghanistan pose real challenges to traditional civilian aid delivery models and principles when state building, rather than emergency relief and development, is the goal of the effort. Capstick suggests some far-reaching structural solutions for the Afghan mission to achieve the kind of coherence needed, but he also cautions that structural solutions alone will not help without a sincere, unified effort by all parties, something that is currently lacking.

Stephen Cornish's perspective comes from decades spent working in conflict areas with humanitarian organizations that include Médecins Sans Frontières and the Canadian Red Cross, as well as his current role as Policy and Advocacy Advisor at CARE Canada. He maintains that the current constructs for civil-military integration, in the form of integrated missions and whole-of-government approaches by donors, while motivated by good intentions, have in fact resulted in humanitarian and development aid programming becoming subordinated to political interests. He notes that aid workers, particularly NGOs, are seen as obstructionist for resisting these integrationist agendas, but they do so because they witness the concrete implications for the protection of civilians and for aid agencies' ability to effectively and equitably meet civilian needs.

He argues that the politicization and militarization of aid that has emerged from a decade of experience with so-called "humanitarian interventions" and that is now so firmly evident in Afghanistan is an issue that should concern policymakers more than it has. He faults the lack of true consultation processes and of a level playing field amongst the three D actors (defence, diplomacy, and development) for resulting policies where, in Afghanistan, the defence D dominates all other agendas. He argues that the evident failures of the 3D effort in Afghanistan are often blamed on what is seen as a "weak and ineffectual" development D and on the unwillingness of NGOs to co-operate with the military, when in fact, the whole integrationist model may be counterproductive for the development gains required to secure stability.

He, like many in the NGO sector, rejects civil-military integration's "ultimate ends" logic, wherein the long-term benefits of peace and protection are realized by sacrificing the current needs for emergency protection and assistance of large segments of the population; he also rejects its attempt to combine inherently incompatible goals. While humanitarian "minimalists" within the NGO community push for classical notions of humanitarian independence and space, "maximalists" are much more comfortable working with governments and foreign militaries in support of long-term state building and conflict transformation. Multi-mandate aid agencies like CARE that combine emergency relief, long-term development aid, and peacebuilding programming find that working in scenarios like Afghanistan poses numerous dilemmas and clear challenges. Looking ahead, Cornish contends that humanitarianism needs to be cordoned off as a separate area independent of 3D thinking, and he makes a strong case for the development D to be treated the same way.

Cedric de Coning is a foremost expert in civil-military coordination policies and practices within UN missions, Cedric de Coning reviews the lessons and challenges highlighted by UN experience and evolving practice on civil-military coordination. His perspective is that the whole civil-military debate has become confused, with the concept of civil-military coordination often misleadingly used to refer to strategic level coherence between the security and development goals of an international peace mission. He outlines how, within contemporary UN peace operations, civil-military coordination (UN CIMIC) is a very specific and very limited body of knowledge centering around liaison between UN military forces and civilian counterparts, providing mission support for external civilian partners such as transport, equipment, and security escorts for humanitarian convoys, as well as providing community support for rehabilitation projects like schools and clinics and reconciliation activities like festivals and sports events.

While this limited function is important in UN missions, he argues it in no way involves the kind of mission-wide strategic planning and coordination at senior levels that aspires to provide system-wide coherence on issues pertaining to the broader security and development agendas.

De Coning also demonstrates that, given the overlap between the roles and functions of civilian and military actors in contemporary UN-integrated missions, security-related tasks such as reform of the security sector or reintegration of excombatants often involve many civilian actors, and that it is impossible to separate civilian and military roles or assets in practical terms. (Existing policies on civil-military and military-humanitarian coordination, he notes, are premised on a clear distinction between civilian and military assets.) Overall, echoing Capstick's observations on Afghanistan, de Coning suggests that established UN guidelines for civil-military coordination and the terms and constructs used in the vigorous debates between the military and the humanitarian sectors are outdated and simply do not apply in the context of current UN peace operation. This presents a clear challenge for civilian humanitarian groups to redefine humanitarian principles in a way that makes sense in this new reality.

Lara Olson and Hrach Gregorian; Finally, our own contribution argues that existing field coordination processes commonly have two main outcomes: either they result in mere "information sharing" and have no real coordination impact, or conversely, they produce a kind of forced "false coherence",[2] referring to superficial changes in language and formal adherence to new frameworks driven by the agenda of the actor with the most power and resources. Either way, the dynamics of field coordination between security- and development-focused agencies has often resulted in frustration and mistrust between these groups, the exact opposite of what was intended.

We outline some key contributors to this problem. Coordination processes often assume agreement among actors about strategies without providing opportunities for inclusive and meaningful multi-stakeholder dialogue. Power asymmetries block real dialogue, and funding relationships and competition limit the ability of existing coordination processes to achieve some level of common intent.

As well, groups hold different notions of the purpose of coordination in the first place, ranging widely from greater centralized control, to democratic consensus building, to credible, reliable information exchange. Furthermore, many NGOs – key implementers of most aid programming in the field – find their engagement with other civilian and military assistance actors results in little to no impact on the broader strategies being pursued, often rendering consultation and consensus building in the field, in their view, "pointless".

We maintain that in working side by side in such settings and preserving their autonomous mandates, roles, and specialized focus, civilian and military agencies can still improve the way their efforts link up and support the bigger peace. Further, the key may be to improve inclusive, two-way communication processes that can help diverse actors define minimum common goals and principles to guide their work. This, in turn, may lay the foundation for better coordination down the road.

While the articles here represent opposing views and perspectives, they are united by a common sense that civil-military coordination is too narrow and limited a construct to frame the relationships and interconnection between the goals of security and development in international peace missions. The broader challenge of aligning these interlinked goals will not be solved by field-based coordination mechanisms and structures alone.

To sum up, current approaches to civil-military coordination suggest a "rowing team" analogy where everyone on the "team" just needs to "pull in the same direction". However, as the authors featured here effectively illustrate, it turns out that some don't remember joining the team, don't want to be on the boat, and refuse to row. Other members will co-operate if the boat is moving in one direction, but not if it turns in another. Some members don't like the unruly nature of the team and keep demanding a captain be appointed. Some team members are paddling with their hands, while others use huge, mechanized oars. Some complain that others are not pulling their weight. Some want to get downriver, but don't want to be seen on the boat with the others. Still others feel that everyone would get downriver faster if they split into separate boats. As this analogy shows, achieving more effective linkages between civilian and military assistance efforts is not merely a coordination or leadership problem; it requires more fundamental dialogue across these assistance communities about where the boat is going – and why – and how.

NOTES

1. Generous financial support for this workshop was provided by the Centre for Military and Strategic Studies, the Canadian International Development Agency (CIDA)'s Conference Secretariat, the Department of National Defence's Security and Defence Forum, NATO's Public Diplomacy Division, and several departments of the University of Calgary – the Faculty of Social Sciences, the International Centre, and the Political Science Department. Equally generous in-kind support was extended by the Institute of World Affairs, and many participating agencies covered the time and costs of their personnel.
2. This useful term was first suggested by a participant in the March 2007 workshop – Cheyanne Church, Lecturer in Human Security, Fletcher School, Tufts University, Boston.

A Means to What End? Why Provincial Reconstruction Teams are Peripheral to the Bigger Political Challenges in Afghanistan

Barbara J. Stapleton

Introduction

The civil-military relationship in the political context of Afghanistan since the overthrow of the Taliban has fulfilled a number of functions, not all of them formally acknowledged. From 2002, it was heavily promoted by the international community within and beyond Afghanistan as a key means of facilitating tangible results in reconstruction and development and in so doing, improving the security situation.[1] Moreover, the phased expansion of NATO forces throughout the country from 2003 onwards was primarily conducted via "Provincial Reconstruction Teams" (PRTs), which came to epitomize the civil-military approach in Afghanistan. The first PRT was operational in Gardez, in the east, by January 2003; over four years later, twenty-five PRTs, led by thirteen different nations, were located in provinces throughout the country.

The central assumptions informing the 2002 PRT plan were that reconstruction and development would be a primary means of expanding the central government's authority beyond Kabul and would provide a security dividend. There was no detailed strategic plan for PRTs via which the PRTs were to reach their broadly stated objectives. In examining aspects of the evolution of PRTs in the political context of Afghanistan from 2002 to the present, the author contends that though the PRT plan was premised and sold on its ability to impact, albeit indirectly, security and reconstruction, the PRT contribution was essentially a political one. As the numbers of PRTs increased from the end of 2003, they played an increasing role at provincial levels in helping maintain the momentum of the political transition[2] that followed the overthrow of the Taliban. Following the end of the Bonn Process in 2005, with parliamentary

---

Particulars of Original Publication:
Reprinted with permission of the *Journal of Military and Strategic Studies* (Fall, 2007). Available online from <http://www.jmss.org/2007/2007fall/index.htm>.

and provincial council elections, the PRTs have continued to attempt to bridge the gaps that frequently exist at provincial and district levels of government. The bigger question posed in the paper is whether post-Bonn, the state-building process will prove to be of lasting substance. Arguably, PRT activities enabled the promotion of an appearance of progress, which distracted from the dire state of governance in many provinces, but about which there was little if any political will, either nationally or internationally, to take more effective action.

The civil-military relationship has meant different things to different actors. Assumptions and expectations on the part of the international community informed the central objective of forging greater co-operation at best, or improved coordination at worst, between PRTs and other development actors in Afghanistan in the interests of shoring up Afghanistan's fragile trajectory of recovery. But misunderstandings and tensions between PRTs and other development actors, including the government, have remained.

The goal of a closer relationship between civilian and military actors, both within the structure of the PRT itself and between PRTs and other civilian development actors, was intended to amplify the "effect" on the ground in the ongoing effort to win wider political support for the government. The integration of civil and military activities was also a key component of counterinsurgency strategies.[3] At the same time, the "paradox of development, that actual outcomes and existing behaviour continually contradict the expected scheme of things,"[4] very much applied to Afghanistan, where knowledge based on first hand experience of its localized and complex socio-political landscape was in very short supply.[5] This situation was compounded by a failure both by the Afghan interim and transitional authorities, supported by the international community, to set a clear moral tone by delivering on leading Afghan concerns, which included the absence of the rule of law and the re-establishment of impunity, increasing corruption, and deteriorating levels of human security.

International efforts to bridge the widening security gap via the delivery of reconstruction and development were not only undermined by the worsening security situation but also by the establishment of a vicious, rather than a virtuous, cycle (via the rule of law and better governance) in the early years of the Bonn Process. As forces and actors opposed to the establishment of law, order, and stability prospered and the rule of impunity was restored in the wake of the Taliban's authoritarian rule, the government became mired in a deepening legitimacy crisis, the causes of which lay well beyond the limited capacity and resources of the PRTs to address meaningfully.

The lack of clarity which has surrounded PRTs from the outset has been fostered by the focus on PRT inputs rather than PRT outputs, which so far have not been consistently monitored or evaluated. Neither has the cost effectiveness of PRTs, to date, been measured against comparative transaction costs by other development actors, which includes the government, NGOs, and private contractors. The absence of any cost/benefit analysis left unanswerable the question of whether PRT outcomes matched the improvements in security, reconstruction, and governance claimed for them. But by mid–2007, discussions between the Afghan Ministry of Finance and donors over the need for PRTs to coordinate more effectively with the government's national development strategy, a sense that PRTs had been oversold in terms of overall effect and quality of outcomes, and that the civil-military approach towards development was increasingly geared towards an expanding insurgency rather than towards the long-term development agendas also being supported by donors, were all on the rise.

Background

The obstacles to building a viable polity in Afghanistan, to which international exit strategies were linked, were historic and formidable. Throughout the history of the modern Afghan state, the writ of central government has been both weak and limited in terms of scope, with continuing tension between the central power and regional tribal autonomy. As rulers attempted modernizing reforms in the twentieth century, tensions increased between the Ulema and the educated elite. As the 1990s progressed, these tensions became more pronounced. Splits between the Ulema saw "Islamists largely renounce their modernizing project and toughen their attitude on social issues, at the same time traditionalist movements such as the Taliban became more radical as a result of their contact with transnational movements such as Al-Qa'ida," [6] leading to the setting up of a fundamentalist state.

Abdur Rahman (1880–1901), known as the Iron Amir, is remembered as the most effective centralizer. He spent much of his reign forcibly incorporating tribes and regions into the state. Though he succeeded in forging unity, Abdur Rahman did not dare tackle development, unlike King Amanullah (1919–29), whose attempt to rapidly modernize the country was perceived by the tribes as eroding their autonomy and consequently violently resisted.[7] The subsequent reigns of Nadir Shah (1929–33) and Zahir Shah (1933–73) saw a slower pace of modernization.[8] The last significant move towards democratic process was the Constitutional Period (1963–73). The 1964 Constitution, which guaranteed free elections and a free press, ended with the coup against Zahir Shah by his cousin Sardar Daud in 1973. This ended the experiment with constitutional monarchy and was followed by a marked increase in Soviet influence, particularly over the army. The series of conflicts that resulted in the wake of the 1978 Saur Revolution led by Marxist-influenced army officers ended the status quo ante in which a Pashtun Durrani elite had dominated other tribal and ethnic groups since 1747.

The devastating conflicts that raged intermittently from 1978 on radically altered the mechanisms through which relations between the centre and the periphery had been conducted in ways which are still not fully understood.[9] Community leaders were weakened, which increased the vulnerability of local communities. The collapse of the Afghan central government in 1992 saw military commanders on all sides increasing their power and autonomy and after a long period of preparation, "the age of the warlords had finally begun." [10] Whether the Afghan wars had ended with the collapse of Taliban rule was open to question. At the same time, the persistence of a strong fundamentalist strain demonstrated in any case "the resistance of a substantial section of Afghan society to the liberal model presented under the auspices of international assistance." [11]

Nevertheless, the majority of Afghans appeared to view the Taliban as a dead end in terms of the jobs, better health, and education that they craved. The need for political change in Afghanistan to enable development and a better future was widely accepted at the start of the Bonn Agreement in December 2001. Public expectations, however, were badly managed. These had already been heightened due to Afghan exposure to the role and scope of government, particularly with regard to the provision of healthcare, education, jobs, and infrastructure witnessed, often for the first time, by the millions of rural Afghans who had fled to Iran and Pakistan in the face of Soviet destruction of the rural economy. Expectations had been further raised by international media reports on financial commitments by the international community of what sounded like vast sums of money for Afghanistan's development. This fuelled perceptions that the country would be transformed virtually overnight. Above all else, public support for the establishment of a strong central government was rooted in the belief that this would prevent renewed conflict. Thus the establishment of government control over the means of violence to end the fragmentation of power and facilitate development was an objective supported by the vast majority of Afghans at the outset. Many Afghans hoped that under a leader free of a tainted past, Hamid Karzai, and with the active support of the most powerful countries in the world, the predatory behaviour and short-termism that had characterized past administrations and security forces would finally end. Instead, it was to reach new heights.

The 2001 Bonn Agreement was forged at a conference hosted by the German government in late November. A range of Afghan political actors (excluding the Taliban), representatives of the UN, US, and European governments, and experts on Afghanistan attended. It was not a peace agreement but it constituted, "a road map for the re-establishment of rudimentary state structures," [12] laying out a path for political transition in Afghanistan, which formally culminated in the holding of elections in 2004 and 2005. Under the auspices of the Bonn Process, stability over the long term was to be achieved through a number of concurrent approaches "premised on the recognition that the re-establishment of state capacity would be a slow and laborious process." [13] These included: (re)construction of the country's war-shattered infrastructure; economic development led by the private sector; reform of the public administration; and most crucially, security sector reform (SSR), in which disarmament and demobilization and reintegration (DDR), the creation of a new Afghan army, a reformed police force, judicial reform, and counter-narcotics were all of pivotal importance. But whether these stepping stones would lead to the "end state" that informed international exit strategy rationales depended also on the Afghan administration's commitment and ability to deliver real changes to the very grim lives led by the majority of Afghans.[14]

The absence of Afghan national security forces capable of securing the state's control over the means of violence meant that stabilization depended on the ability of the international community to react swiftly to the security challenges that emerged in the transitional period. Potential responses to the threat that a widening security gap posed to the Bonn Process, such as a regional expansion of the UN-mandated peacekeeping forces in Kabul, were constrained by a number of factors, however. Paramount amongst these was the perceived interests of the US-led coalition in its prosecution of the "war on terror" in southern Afghanistan. But wider international support for the increased levels and types of resources identified by a range of experts as fundamental for building a sustainable stability was not forthcoming.[15]

As the security gap widened, Afghan power realities rapidly moved in directions that fundamentally undermined the democratic processes and structures the Bonn Process was supposed to establish. Resistance to the political reforms on which meaningful progress in SSR depended subjected urgently needed reform processes to long delays.[16] The DDR process, for example, did not start until October 2003, following long awaited reforms to the Ministry of Defence. Hence, political reforms that were a prerequisite to the holding of free and fair elections were only partially underway with less than a year to go before the 2004 presidential elections.

Insecurity also slowed the pace of reconstruction while significantly increasing its cost both in the field and in Kabul, where the presence of private security companies was ever more visible. The foreign investors needed to develop the private sector and provide jobs were frightened off.[17] Most damaging of all, as the trade in opium was re-established, it fuelled corruption at district, provincial, and central levels of government, allowing increasingly organized criminal syndicates to co-opt the administration where it counted, in the interests of facilitating opium cultivation and trafficking. Finally, regional commanders and other local power holders who had been weakened or had disappeared under the Taliban regime were able to restore and strengthen their positions effectively unopposed. The resurgence of "warlordism" was also facilitated by the coalition's strategy of using Afghan militias in the prosecution of the war on terror.[18] To the growing disillusionment of the Afghan people, individuals strongly suspected of being involved in the drugs trade and to have been involved in serious human rights violations in the past and/or present were placed in official positions of power provincially and within the central government. Significantly, many Afghan professionals in the Diaspora chose not to return. The sharp surges in poppy cultivation from 2002 onwards continued to reflect the absence of law and order.

THE POLITICAL CONTEXT TO THE LAUNCH OF THE PRT PLAN

The international community's difficulty in reconciling its key agendas in Afghanistan – the war on terror and the state-building process – was apparent in the UN Security Council's decision not to amend the International Security Assistance Force's (ISAF) mandate which limited the force to Kabul and its immediate surrounds. Urgent calls for an increase in ISAF numbers and its expansion regionally were repeatedly made in 2002 by the head of the UN mission, Lakhdar Brahimi, and the interim president, Hamid Karzai. Early US opposition to ISAF's expansion was determinant, however, as the US alone possessed the air resources, in-country, on which any European-manned expansion would rely.[19] Possible causes underlying the US position were thought at the time to derive from American fears that a regional presence of peacekeeping forces could obstruct coalition operations against al-Qa'ida and what the coalition referred to as "the remnants of the Taliban" in addition to increasing the chances of "friendly fire" incidents. In the event, the US administration's attention had already moved elsewhere, and important US military assets had been moved out of Afghanistan by the latter half of 2002 in preparation for the decision, apparently made shortly after the September 11 terrorist attacks, to invade Iraq.[20]

By mid-2002, concern that the state-building process was already slipping out of the control of the main donors who sponsored it was growing. This drove the development of an alternative plan to expand the coalition's civil-military affairs strategy (hitherto a component in the coalition's counterinsurgency strategy in the south), to the rest of the country via "Joint Regional Teams", the forerunners to PRTs. The plan's objectives were broadly stated: to extend the legitimacy and authority of the central government beyond Kabul and to facilitate reconstruction, thereby improving the overall security situation. The plan's architects included British as well as American coalition representatives in Kabul. The PRTs, which merged security and development, were intended to provide temporary support to the Afghan authorities – to buy time in which government capacity could be developed and in which attempts to get meaningful progress in the reform process as a whole (prior to the presidential elections scheduled for June 2004) could be renewed.

The PRTs were comprised of joint civil-military teams initially numbering fifty to one-hundred military personnel geared to the provision of "force protection" and the protection of the civil-military reservists who provided the reconstruction and development expertise. From 2003 onwards, civilian development and political experts from the American and European governments were embedded in PRTs in what became standard practice. Though it was claimed that security in the PRT area of operation would improve by virtue of the PRTs' presence, PRTs were never mandated, constructed, or intended to afford direct protection to Afghan civilians or, for that matter, other development actors.[21] In extremis, PRTs could rely on the ability to "reach-back" to coalition air power.

That the PRT plan had been initially oversold by coalition spokesmen was acknowledged by the coalition in its report to UNAMA in the only evaluation of PRTs conducted.[22] The long shopping list of skills and resources that PRTs would bring into Afghanistan mostly never materialized. Instead, the PRT approach continued to revolve around quick impact projects (QIPs), which focused on the visible, minor reconstruction activities intended to win friends quickly and garner valuable information, in line with counterinsurgency strategy. Given that some of the QIPs resembled the humanitarian projects undertaken by NGOs, the expansion of the military's involvement in humanitarian-type activities was bound to be highly controversial amongst the assistance sector. To the surprise of incoming military rotations, the expansion in civil-military affairs proved far more controversial in Afghanistan with the assistance community than the military's earlier involvement in humanitarian crises in Iraqi Kurdistan and Kosovo. The role of the military in providing resources in the short term to relieve humanitarian crises and/or provide security allowing humanitarian agencies to act was relatively straightforward. The highly complex operating environment of Afghanistan, where US-led coalition forces were also on a war footing, was another matter.

As PRTs were going to go ahead with or without them, some NGOs decided to engage in policy discussions over PRT approaches. This process was led in Kabul by the NGO umbrella organization ACBAR (Agency Coordinating Body for Afghan Relief), which had been established in Peshawar in 1988 when NGOs were the gateway to the provision of assistance to the Afghan people. ACBAR sought to limit effects perceived as potentially harmful to NGO security and to the future operational capacity of NGOs, given the uncertainty of the political future. Some NGOs, such as Medecins sans Frontieres, did not publicly engage in these discussions due to a policy of keeping a strict separation from anything connected to the military in an effort to preserve humanitarian space. Other NGOs, along with UNAMA and UN agencies, viewed PRTs more pragmatically against a security situation that was already reducing access to increasing areas of the south, while in the north, competing warlords periodically engaged in clashes. NGO and UN support for the plan at the time was largely predicated on the absence of any other response by the international community to address the widening security gap during the transitional period when the Afghan government lacked sufficient security forces.

Against this background, the announcement of the PRT plan was welcomed by the Afghan Transitional Authority and UNAMA as a sign at least of continuing engagement by the international community as Afghanistan's problems intensified.[23] But this announcement effectively closed the door on any timely expansion of UN-mandated peacekeeping forces to regional urban centres. This had been expected by the Afghan people following ISAF's stabilization of Kabul in early 2002. The calls made for ISAF's expansion in 2002 had been actively supported by the UN, academics, and some international NGOs, as expediting reconstruction depended on sufficient levels of security being established as soon as possible. Instead, the expansion of a civil-military approach was presented as a means to help facilitate the delivery of reconstruction and development, which in turn would confer stability. As critics dismissed the poorly resourced PRTs as an attempt to provide the ISAF effect on the cheap,[24] the plan's defenders in UNAMA and the coalition saw the PRTs as a matter of doing something with the limited resources available, given that nothing else was on offer.[25] The underlying hope expressed privately by one senior UN representative at the time was that PRTs might prove to be a means to draw in, albeit gradually, greater numbers of international forces which would help to stabilize the country.

THE ABSENCE OF A PRT MANDATE

While PRT activities evolved, the absence of a detailed mandate spelling out exactly how the PRT's key objective, the expansion of the central government's legitimacy and authority, would be achieved, remained. Any critique of this state of affairs was countered by the coalition and later ISAF on the basis that PRTs needed flexibility in order to be effective in the diverse operating environments they functioned in. A detailed mandate, it was argued, would act as a constraint. The rejection of a "one-size-fits-all" approach for PRTs in this regard was understandable. But it also obviated the need to define a strategic and coherent, PRT-specific response to the actual challenges to the state-building project, which were all too apparent in the uncoordinated and slow progress being made in security sector reform. Confusion over the purpose of PRTs could only continue under these circumstances, while PRT approaches were essentially reactive and ad hoc. In addition, PRT operations were also subject to manipulation by provincial governors as well as the whims of successive military commanders who conducted PRT operations as they saw fit. At best, PRTs amounted to a form of crisis management but one that allowed the political implications of the crisis confronted to be avoided, in the short term at any rate.

The rationale for the PRTs' central role, the extension of the central government's authority, was based on a simplistic categorization of the actors involved and an underestimation of the sophistication of the political challenges confronted. Kabul-based line ministries were perceived as the "good guys"; their provincial counterparts required training, and non-state actors were labeled the "bad guys". Thus, the deployment of the PRTs into the provinces to capacity build the local administration in theory would link the provinces to the centre. But the situation was far more complex than that, especially in the socio-political sphere where distinctions and allegiances were notoriously fluid. The central government was in many respects as dysfunctional as the provinces, and progress in the provinces, especially with respect to good governance, was very often blocked by ministries within the central government itself.

Though critics of the PRTs highlighted the absence of a detailed mandate in obscuring their purpose and actual achievements, others interpreted this situation as a welcome state of "constructive ambiguity." [26] Conceivably, the advantages of ambiguity were related to the coalition and US government's active encouragement to hesitant NATO member states to either take over existing PRTs or establish new ones.[27] In any event, PRT activities could be cited by coalition spokesmen in the management of perceptions (both internally and externally) as increasingly negative media reports surfaced about the slow progress of reconstruction and worsening security in Afghanistan.

The Attempt to Establish a Unified PRT Approach

By mid-2003, the political constraints responsible for the largely stalled security sector reform (SSR) process had led to increasing calls from donors for PRTs to support security sector reform (SSR) more actively, particularly in the realms of disarmament and demobilization. A shift in PRT focus was also under consideration by the US embassy, which had issued civil-military guidelines in this period that emphasized projects for local government as well as PRT involvement in heavy infrastructure projects.[28] This encouraged hopes that efforts then being led by UNAMA to get a unified PRT approach would succeed in diverting PRTs away from minor reconstruction projects towards security sector reform.

In consultations with the coalition and a few international NGOs, UNAMA identified priority areas where PRTs could maximize their comparative advantage, namely in areas where NGOs could not operate, such as rebuilding customs houses, courthouses, and police and other local administrative buildings. To the degree that this strategy was implemented, it was argued, this would also bring PRTs closer to the key objective of expanding the central government's authority. A number of other interests would be met by this shift: preventing the duplication of activities already being carried out by NGOs; raising the central government's profile while strengthening its ability to function provincially; contributing to an enabling security environment in which professional development actors could access communities; and to the extent that this shift was implemented, it would decrease the grounds for blurring the boundaries between the military and humanitarian sectors.

The British PRT set up in Mazar e Sharif in July 2003 was expected to lead the way, with New Zealand following suit via its PRT in Bamyan. In preparing its PRT approach, the British Ministry of Defense had consulted widely with UN agencies and NGOs. Promises made not to duplicate in any way the work of NGOs were largely kept. Most importantly in the eyes of many observers, the focus was to be on improving security. This was manifested in regular patrolling of the hinterland well off the beaten track as well as focusing resources on raising levels of professional policing. Projects were selected that strengthened the infrastructure of government provincially, in contrast to building schools, wells, and clinics, which continued to characterize PRT approaches elsewhere. But despite the PRT's contribution to the success of UN-led mediation efforts between clashing northern commanders in 2003,[29] PRT activities in the region ultimately amounted to crisis management. Since the British PRT was not mandated or resourced to address security challenges directly, it could not fundamentally alter the power realities that had re-emerged following the collapse of the Taliban, which were obstructing the state-building process and security sector reform. Though a partial shift in focus towards SSR occurred in coalition-led PRTs, it did not turn into the total shift argued for by the UN at the time.

Afghan NGOs did not contribute significantly to the debate on coordinating civilian and military approaches to the development challenges confronted in Afghanistan in the early years of the Bonn Process. Concepts such as humanitarian space were not then a leading concern. A more pressing urgency was the fact that the funding environment had become much tougher for NGOs, as donors stopped directly funding them and instead channeled development funding through the central government and UN agencies. For Afghan NGOs, many of which bore more resemblance to private contractors, PRTs represented a potential source of funding. Beyond these considerations, concrete results were what counted most. As an Afghan colleague who had spent thirty years working in development put it, "the Afghans want the apple and they don't care if it comes from the apple or the willow tree."

THE EVOLUTION OF THE PRT PLAN

The deployment of the initial PRTs in early 2003 was officially linked to the coalition's simultaneous announcement that it was moving from Phase III (stabilization of Afghanistan) into Phase IV (reconstruction), which enabled military resources to be diverted from the war on terror to reconstruction and development. From this period on, the coalition tended to refer to the situation in the south as a counterinsurgency rather than as a part of the war on terror.

From the outset, PRTs had been officially linked to keeping the ambitious Bonn Process on track, particularly with regard to holding presidential and parliamentary elections, scheduled for 2004 and 2005 respectively. At the launch of the PRT plan in November 2002, PRTs were heralded as a means to "build the Afghan Transitional Authority's legitimacy and authority as we move towards the elections." [30] But by mid-2003, only four PRTs were in existence and these were restricted by minimal and slow-moving funding lines.

At a meeting with NGOs in mid-2003 in Kabul, coalition General Karl Eikenberry had described the PRTs as "an empty vessel." However, a few months later, this situation was transformed with the arrival of General Barno (who took over command of coalition forces) and Zalmay Khalilzad (the new US ambassador) in Kabul. Hitherto, the US had been detached from the state-building process, but US attitudes sharply reversed[31] with the inception of the Accelerate Success Programme, run from the US embassy under Ambassador Khalilzad. Barno particularly focused on PRTs, and numbers and funding lines were rapidly increased. By December 2003, a PRT was operational in Kandahar in the south. In the first quarter of 2004, the US military had stood up PRTs in Jalalabad, Assadabad, Ghazni, Khost, and Qalat, the provincial capitals of provinces in the south-east and east, neighbouring Pakistan.

As indicated, the evolution of the PRT plan took place against a security situation that was the subject of conflicting claims. International media reports repeatedly emphasized the US administration's need for a foreign policy success story in Afghanistan to offset the unraveling disaster in Iraq as the Bush administration prepared for re-election in 2004. Concurrently, Taliban successes in the south were continually dismissed at press briefings by the coalition and US officials visiting Afghanistan as signs that the insurgency was in its death throes. At press briefings throughout 2004, General Barno often referred to the PRTs, explicitly linking them to the establishment of what he termed the achievement of "enduring security" in Afghanistan – though the measures that would bring about this end state were never described. Senior officers of non-US military interviewed by the author at the time, however, viewed the civil-military approach of the PRTs as standard military practice dating back to counterinsurgency strategies developed by the British army in Borneo and Malaya in the 1950s and 1960s.

As PRTs, along with all other available assets, were utilized to prepare the ground for the presidential elections in Afghanistan, due a few months prior to the US elections, the US ambassador led the international community in a determined push to maintain the Bonn momentum and hold Afghan elections on schedule, despite the security risks involved.[32] Ultimately, the increased security measures taken by NATO, the coalition, and Afghan security forces helped ensure that, though flawed in terms of process, the elections had a positive outcome. The Afghan people showed great bravery in overcoming the fear and intimidation liberally spread beforehand by political opponents of the electoral process and turned out in large numbers at the polling booths. In the wake of a majority vote for Hamid Karzai and the Taliban's failure to disrupt the electoral process as they had publicly sworn to do, the US government was able to legitimize its earlier claims that the coalition's intervention in Afghanistan was a democratic success story and that Afghanistan represented "the good war".

As PRTs increased in number, the structure of the teams changed. The numbers of civil affairs personnel decreased and the embedding of USAID and US State Department representatives to advise on development and local politics became the norm. Concurrently, the numbers of infantry protecting civilian advisers increased. After months of delay, the Afghan Ministry of Interior began to send civilian representatives to join the teams. The previously "empty" PRT vessel was also filled in terms of financial resources. The US Congress effectively doubled the budget for Afghanistan for the US funding year 2004, which totaled over two billion dollars. Half of the budget was designated for the improvement of security; the funding priorities being the development of the Afghan

National Army and the Ministry of Defense. Smaller sums were directed at equipping and training police and counter-narcotics activities. Fifty-two million dollars were allocated for the PRTs, the majority of which was designated for their projects.

Increased funding was channeled via three budget lines now available to the coalition. The existing Overseas Humanitarian Disaster and Civic Assistance (OHDACA) line under the US Department of Defense was joined by the US State Department's Emergency Support Funds. A totally new budget line, the Commander's Emergency Reconstruction Programme (CERP), allowed PRT commanders to draw on one hundred thousand dollars a month for projects, virtually at their discretion. This development in particular dismayed UNAMA, which was then attempting to divert PRT focus towards the security sector reform processes mentioned earlier in the paper.

THE ART OF THE POSSIBLE

The comparatively large amounts of funding at the disposal of US PRT commanders and the additional funding controlled by embedded USAID representatives distinguished PRTs based in the south from the British- and New Zealand-led PRTs in the north and centre. The British government, for example, made approximately just one million pounds available to its development adviser in the Mazar-e-Sharif PRT in 2004. But approaches that had focused on extensive patrols of the northern hinterland, professionalization of the police, and reconstruction projects linked to the restoration of the administrative infrastructure that had proved viable in the north, did not survive the subsequent British PRT transfer to the south, where more complex socio-political conditions obtained.

The British departure from Mazar to take over the PRT in Helmand in April 2006, a province then largely under the control of anti-government forces, saw a marked increase in funding through the PRT for development and quick impact projects.[33] The British Ministry of Defence (MoD) also introduced a "CERPs equivalent" fund of 40,000 pounds per month for the military. These funds were controlled by the lead military representative in the PRT, and they had to be spent monthly or be forfeited. In practice, this mechanism, internal to the MoD, was where the "hearts and minds" projects were funded from. Such funding arrangements (employed on a much larger scale by the US Department of Defense[34]), had been viewed as inappropriate by the British MoD for its PRT in the north in the past. Reconstruction and development projects, apart from an initial phase linked to the establishment of force protection, had been discarded there. The funding changes that followed the British PRT move to Helmand in the south reflected the perceived exigencies of the insurgency, in which the delivery of QIPs was central to "force protection" considerations. But these new funding arrangements were at odds with the establishment by the British of a civilian lead for the Helmand PRT and the recognition of the overriding need for long-term approaches if development was to be meaningful and sustainable.

The increase in PRT funding had allowed the US-led PRTs in the south to widen their range of projects. By 2005, these included increased support to the police and basic management training for local government, as well as workshops on narcotics. However, the rolling CERP funds ensured the continued provision of quick impact projects (QIPs). Apart from counterinsurgency considerations, QIPs had the advantage of providing fast, visible, and quantifiable results. The numbers of schools, clinics, and wells built could be promoted both to the Afghan public and to policy-makers in Kabul and Washington. However, the provision of skilled staff needed for the functioning of schools and clinics was beyond the remit and resources of PRTs. Decades of experience had demonstrated to NGOs that oversight was vital to ensure decent construction outcomes in Afghanistan, where contractors will often try to cut costs and use the cheapest building materials available unless closely monitored. These problems were overcome by PRTs in areas where a partnership existed with professional NGOs[35] that could provide the human resources required and support the community in the maintenance of whichever school or clinic had been constructed via PRT funds. Less frequently, this was also the case where a competent government line ministry was present.

Reports of PRT-funded schools and clinics being built without teachers and medics to staff them continued to surface, however, leading to criticism from the Afghan government as well as from NGOs. Lessons learned in this regard were identified.[36] However, the government's concern that the PRTs amounted to a parallel development strategy outside its financial control was reflected in an intermittent critique that surfaced in meetings between the government and donors over the years. In particular, PRTs were criticized for failing to coordinate sufficiently over national development strategies, either at the centre or via line ministry representatives in the provinces. In reality, the PRTs could find almost no effective counterparts in many sectors at the provincial or district levels with whom they might coordinate.

The external as well as internal pressures on PRT commanders to get results on the ground fast often led to substandard outcomes. In 2005, a US civil-military reservist in the Gardez PRT in the south-east described the "uniformly poor" results of building work contracted out by the PRT to local companies in Paktia and the Paktika provinces, stating, "you could put your feet through the sidewalk." According to a UNAMA representative recently interviewed by the author, this situation has not significantly improved in the south-east. In addition to insufficient oversight, the brevity of military rotations,[37] and the tendency of new PRT commanders to want to make their own mark via projects started under their watch also militated against continuity.

The main critique of the military's involvement in development work was that rather than being needs based (which referred to the core humanitarian principles of assistance being based on neutrality, impartiality and independence claimed by NGOs), it was based on military and political objectives. However, many NGO activities in Afghanistan were also donor driven and similarly tied to overall political objectives. Some NGOs were able to utilize funding for Afghanistan from separate sources in an effort to retain independence. But most NGOs were not in a position to choose and had little option but to become implementing partners in the Afghan government's development plans, some of which, such as the National Solidarity Programme, had distinct political overtones.

In the aftermath of the 2004 presidential elections, debates about the value added by PRTs ended. The PRTs had helped deliver a positive outcome provincially, and the concept was validated in the eyes of donors and government. Plans to place a PRT in all thirty-four provinces developed apace as the subject of PRTs continued to take up increasing amounts of political space in Washington and Brussels. As numbers of PRTs increased throughout 2004, the utility of PRTs in providing eyes and ears for donors unable to access increasing areas of the country was obvious. PRTs also provided a secure "bed and breakfast" for the troop-contributing nations' development and political advisers and for visiting dignitaries. The involvement of PRTs in bridging provincial development and governance needs maintained a sense of momentum and became central to policy discussions in Kabul.

More Cooks in the Kitchen

In the second half of 2003, Britain, New Zealand, and Germany stood up or took over the lead of PRTs under coalition command.[38] The German takeover of the Kunduz PRT in the north followed the UN Security Council's adjustment to ISAF's mandate in September 2003, which finally permitted ISAF's expansion beyond Kabul. Germany had led diplomatic efforts to secure the adjustment, which allowed the Kunduz PRT to transfer to NATO command. This was an important consideration for the German government, given the strength of domestic opposition to the war in Iraq. Although a shift towards security had been implemented by the British and New Zealand PRTs in the north and centre of Afghanistan, the attempt to establish a universal PRT model had not transpired. Instead, the PRTs' broadly stated objectives and lack of mandate favoured the emergence of different national interpretations of PRTs to varying ends. Indeed, many NATO member states would not have become involved had it been otherwise.

The German PRT approach, which focused on visible development projects, departed from the more direct approaches towards security taken by the British and New Zealanders. A risk-adverse approach adopted by the German government was evident in the choice of its PRT location in Kunduz, then considered a relatively "benign" area where security was not adversely affecting the implementation of development programmes by NGOs and UN Agencies. The German PRT proved a harbinger of the disparate national approaches that would proliferate as NATO/ISAF expanded. The German government's refusal to allow direct PRT engagement in narcotics-related issues would also be emulated by many NATO troop-contributing nations.[39] This confused observers because poppy cultivation was the main problem that existed in Kunduz at that time.

The May 2003 joint assessment of the first three PRTs facilitated by UNAMA to inform directions of future PRTs, had included representatives from UN agencies and NGOs as well as the coalition. A number of points were agreed to by the assistance community in a subsequent report: That it was too early to judge whether PRTs would prove to be a contributory factor in support of the Bonn Process or not; that any PRT contribution would depend on the extent that PRTs shifted focus away from minor reconstruction projects to building government administrative capacity at the district and provincial levels, as well as the facilitation of the deployment and civic-action activities of the Afghan national army and the national police; that the absence of government representatives in the PRT process undermined the PRT's main objective – to expand Kabul's legitimacy and authority; and finally, that in view of the deteriorating security situation, PRTs should support the establishment of greater security in Afghanistan by supporting security sector reform and DDR in particular.

More controversially, the report stated that the PRTs' ability to undertake traditional assistance activities in areas too insecure for non-military actors to operate was "welcomed" by the UN participants. This was challenged at the time by NGOs who had succeeded in maintaining programmes in insecure areas in Afghanistan. They argued that the international community's failure to address the rising levels of violence in Afghanistan was the determining factor in preventing NGO access, and consequently assistance, to increasing numbers of Afghan children, women, and men in some of the poorest areas of the country. But despite the comparative advantages held by PRTs, their resources were not concentrated in the high-risk, marginalized districts that often comprised the very areas targeted by insurgents. Instead, PRT projects, like the PRTs, tended to be located in provincial centres and the immediate surrounds.

In other cases, situating projects in contested areas was considered too dangerous for PRTs, which were essentially geared towards, and promoted to domestic publics as, a contribution towards peacekeeping operations. Further factors that contributed to the tendency for the PRTs to focus efforts on the towns included ease of access, and in particular, the close working relationship that the PRT commander developed with the provincial governor. The governor, based in the provincial capital, probably only visited the more remote and insecure districts of his province once or twice a year. Visits were usually facilitated and encouraged by the PRT. The governor would be biased anyway towards locating politically legitimizing projects in the provincial centre or where his own tribal or ethnic group was located.

PRTs brought significant resources with them, which provided considerable leverage to governors. Consequently, every governor was very keen to have one. The remote and extremely poor provinces, such as Ghor, depended on the efforts of the handful of NGOs able to maintain a presence due to funding from the European Community Humanitarian Office (ECHO) or as implementing partners in rather insecure Afghan government development programmes.[40] For such provinces, a PRT presence represented a lifeline to chances of significant reconstruction and development projects being funded and implemented.

THE QUESTION OF ACCESS

Towards the latter half of 2003, increasing areas of the south-west were assessed as "high risk" and coloured red on the UN security accessibility maps that were regularly updated. Red denoted areas inaccessible to UN agency staff. The ability of leading development NGOs to maintain programme delivery increasingly depended on the efforts of locally recruited staff, some of whom had been networked into communities in Helmand and Kandahar provinces for over twenty years. Though international military forces tended to view NGOs as autonomous actors, it was the Afghan communities themselves that determined whether local NGO staff could continue to work with them or not. The only exception to this dynamic was if the NGO in question had links to local Taliban networks, which might allow some projects to go ahead. Up to 2005, such considerations were largely determined by the ability of the community in question to offer security to the NGO working with them. As the insurgency expanded and the government proved unable to offer protection, the question of whether the community could afford to be seen to be associated with NGOs dominated. "Going local" allowed NGOs to maintain programmes but significantly limited the range of programming to those that could be run effectively from a distance.

To reach communities, NGOs had to travel by roads. "Show me where the roads end, and I will show you where the Taliban begins," General Eikenberry was reportedly fond of telling his staff.[41] But the lack of security trumped the economic benefits that resulted from new roads, initially in the south and subsequently in other parts of the country. The deterioration in road security in the south, which increased from 2004, was a key factor driving the NGO retraction of programming to provincial capitals, if not a closure of programmes altogether. A series of ACBAR press releases issued throughout the latter half of 2003 highlighted security incidents, which mainly occurred on the roads. By the end of that year, ACBAR was reporting rising numbers of fatal attacks against NGO staff, a phenomenon that was to increase with every passing year.[42] The complex factors fuelling insecurity were reflected in the limited investigations made into security incidents. These often revealed links to local criminal elements and banditry, factional disputes, and the actions of local officials as well as those by anti-government forces.[43] By the end of 2006, with insecurity erupting in the north and west, aid agencies were limiting and closing programmes in parts of Farah, Badghis, and Faryab provinces.

CIVIL–MILITARY ATTEMPTS TO SQUARE THE SECURITY CIRCLE

The challenges inherent to the security situation were epitomized in Kandahar City where, in addition to the terrorist threat, at least five militias and police forces jockeyed for position under the control of different tribal leaders. This mirrored the security conditions that had led to the original rise of the Taliban in 1994. Following a series of security incidents targeting UNHCR and UNAMA in 2004, a new plan to win back the south was announced at a meeting with NGOs and UN agencies in Kandahar by coalition and UN representatives. It was called the Provincial Stabilisation Strategy (PSS).

The objective of the PSS was to provide urgently needed reconstruction in the form of roads and water to dangerous areas that had become inaccessible to UN agencies and NGOs. With their ability to call in coalition air power, PRTs were at the heart of a security package tailored to facilitate leadership by properly trained Afghan police (as opposed to the militia forces, called "police" in Kandahar), and augmented by local authorities loyal to the central government. The inclusion of good governance for the first time was notable in that it reflected growing international concern in this regard. The plan was test run in two areas of Kandahar Province, Shah Wali Kot in the north and Shurabak near the border with Pakistan. If successful, the approach would be implemented in other parts of the south where the government was losing control. Almost one year later, however, there was little to show for the plan. The root causes of failure were identified by a USAID representative who had directly observed its implementation as "an inability to include a viable security plan or to commit sufficient resources of the right kind fast enough." Nevertheless, the PSS, re-labeled as Regional Development Zones (RDZ), was widely referred to in military briefings and in policy discussions in Kabul many months after the concept had ceased to have any relevance on the ground.

In 2006, ISAF IX used similar ingredients to the PSS in the promotion of Afghan Development Zones that were established around provincial capitals in the south. As development and governance improved within them, the theory went, ADZs would expand like ink blots and gradually join up. A key difference from the PSS approach was that the ADZs followed major military operations, such as Operation Medusa in Kandahar Province, which had cleared insurgents out of the areas targeted. However, the inability of the Afghan police to hold ground cleared led to military gains being effectively transient. Over a year later, the ADZs had not made significant headway and were rarely referred to.

It is interesting to compare the civil-military approaches outlined above with UNAMA's success in squaring the security circle from 2005 onwards in a tribal region known as the Zadran Arc, which spanned the three south-eastern provinces that make up Loya Paktia. Historically, this region had been far less penetrated by the state, and coherent tribal structures remained in control of distinct geographical areas, unlike the south, where tribal structures were far more fragmented. UNAMA acted on the political opportunity that the distinct tribal landscape in the south-east presented. The Zadran Arc was rated as high risk by the UN[44] and had received very little reconstruction assistance since the fall of the Taliban. Like earlier attempts outlined above, UNAMA's approach also combined security, governance, and reconstruction elements, but UNAMA was able to achieve a durable tribal consensus via the inclusion of all the Zadran sub and sub-sub tribes in prior consultations.

The Zadran Arc Stabilisation Initiative was signed by the three provincial governors concerned. It promised the delivery of development projects chosen by the tribes against the provision of tribal security. An immediate cessation of development would follow if any attacks on projects occurred. UNAMA had already secured the funds for the agreed projects and was in a position to deliver on promises made. The trust and confidence engendered has led to further requests for UNAMA to mediate with anti-government elements to allow major development projects, such as the sixty million dollar Gardez to Khost road, to proceed. The maintenance of oversight and ongoing consultations between tribal representatives and UNAMA proved vital to the success of a process which the socio-political conditions of the south-east had made possible.

In August 2007, PRT engagement in Helmand in the south-west included reconstruction projects following destructive military operations in Sangin and Greshk as well as attempts to develop the capacity of sub-national administrations in the delivery of services and sustainable development. Progress in implementing the latter was hampered though, both by a security situation where threat levels were so high[45] that civilian advisers were restricted from leaving the PRT and by a local administration described as "a mixture of the incompetent, illiterate and criminal." [46]

Major counterinsurgency operations had been launched the previous year in Kandahar Province against hundreds of insurgents that threatened the politically symbolic city of Kandahar. A number of operations were launched, which culminated in Operation Medusa in Panjwai and Zhare districts in September, to clear Taliban fighters from these strategic areas. NATO claimed that 1,500 insurgents were killed in the operation, which involved aerial bombardment, and an estimated 80,000 Afghans were displaced. In the wake of this operation, NATO forces moved into Panjwai "with bricks, bulldozers and lots of cash" in an effort to regain peoples' trust.[47] According to Afghan sources, these operations temporarily restored peoples' confidence. But within one year the insurgents had returned, illustrating again the inability of the police to hold ground cleared. The situation was described by one US journalist as part of "a bloody stalemate" between NATO forces and Taliban fighters across southern Afghanistan.[48] In a recent interview with an Afghan researcher based in Kandahar, the situation in the south was also referred to as "a stalemate" and one that reportedly people increasingly felt could not be tolerated for much longer. "People don't care if the roads built are paved with gold; they would rather have security," I was told.[49]

PRTs AND PROVINCIAL GOVERNANCE

In Afghanistan, the "plan" can substitute for the action. As reform processes came up against the political constraints that often rendered them ineffectual, the tendency was to start another process and abandon the former one. Alternatives to this would have required a unified effort by leading donors to make existing processes work by identifying and agreeing on the underlying problems, at central as well as provincial and district government levels, that held reform processes hostage and then committing the necessary resources needed to effectively confront them. No such unified approach has been taken regarding counter-narcotics, DIAG, or police reform. The attempts to develop competent provincial governance structures have similarly reflected the ad hoc, reactive, and piecemeal approaches that too often have characterized the post-Taliban international engagement in Afghanistan.

Despite its failure, the Regional Development Zone concept influenced the development of Provincial Development Committees (PDCs), which amounted to an economic cabinet for the provincial governor attended by provincial line ministry representatives. This structure added to the existing and emerging plethora of coordination mechanisms at provincial and district levels from late 2004. These coordination structures had developed in response to the donors' need to establish effective mechanisms for development at provincial and district levels, as the majority of development funding remained trapped in Kabul due to limited government absorptive capacity at all levels.[50] In addition, the 2005 parliamentary elections would change, in theory at least, the structures, processes, and politics of sub-national government in Afghanistan via the elected Provincial Councils. Concerns were raised by March 2005 over the danger that poorly funded and badly supported elected bodies with an unclear role would be the result, and that the duplication of provincial coordination structures, which included the PRTs, only added to the overall confusion.[51]

From late 2004, the subject of PDCs had been central to discussions at the weekly meetings of the PRT Working Group[52] in Kabul. The initiative had been formulated in response to government concerns, publicly voiced by the then Minister of Finance, Ashraf Ghani, that the PRTs were a law unto themselves. The PRT Executive Steering Committee, which authorized PRT policy and was comprised of ambassadors of PRT-contributing nations, relevant members of the Afghan Cabinet, and ISAF and coalition representatives, was tasked to examine the alignment of PRTs within the Afghan government's national coordination strategy for development, the National Priority Programs (NPPs). The PRT Working Group that prepared the agenda for PRT ESC meetings was convinced that the PDC concept being developed would provide a mechanism to accelerate provincial development and governance. Theoretically, this was to be achieved by the inclusion of community *shuras* in the PDCs to ensure community "ownership" of the development process. The fact that government at district and provincial levels often tended to be either ineffective to the point of being non-existent or was co opted by criminal networks was not publicly commented on during these discussions, underlining the increasingly surreal disjuncture between policy discussions on aspirations to extend central government control and the reality on the ground.

By 2005, the Interim Afghanistan National Development Strategy (IANDS) had replaced National Priority Programmes as the government's master plan for development. It included the World Bank requirement for a Poverty Reduction Strategy Paper (PRSP), which was a precondition for International Finance Institution funding strategies. But government plans for urgently needed reforms both to sub-national governance and provincial administrations – in line with the vision laid out by the government in the IANDS – remained unclear. Analysts highlighted the need for increased attention and strong political leadership if reforms were to succeed.[53] In particular, the task of coordinating provincial planning activity and resolving the question of how elected but powerless provincial councils were to feed into these processes remained unresolved.

The IANDS informed the Afghanistan Compact agreed to in London in January 2006 by the Afghan government and donors. It framed relations between them following the ending of the Bonn Process. The full ANDS included a requirement for sub-national consultations with provincial council and other civil society representatives at district and provincial levels over provincial development plans. The PRTs played the main facilitating role in this process in many areas, illustrating both the absence of other development actors and the limits of provincial government capacity. Where good governors and an active provincial council existed in addition to UNAMA representation, PRT involvement was less of a necessity.

The military is trained to identify and fill gaps. The *US Army Counterinsurgency Field Manual* states, "The organizing imperative is focusing on what needs to be done not on who does it." [54] Such attitudes are at odds with meaningful capacity building, which in Afghanistan will require time above all other factors. A recent World Bank report widely seen as critical of the involvement of PRTs in governance as well as development at provincial levels, summarized the critical dilemma "confronted and constituted" by PRTs – "in trying to create the space for the Afghan state to develop and cohere they run the risk of undermining it." [55]

NATO's Expansion and the Insurgency

The phased expansion of ISAF forces from late 2003 to 2006 proved a difficult and very slow process[56] as well as a highly controversial one due to the likelihood of NATO forces being involved in kinetic operations in the south. The costly business of setting up the mandatory forward support bases, which included medical and air support, was one factor delaying the NATO plan to roll out PRTs. But the entire process was repeatedly delayed by the unwillingness of some NATO member states to commit sufficient resources in a timely fashion, despite having signed up to the overriding NATO mission in Afghanistan. Security plans for elections in 2004 and 2005 were predicated on the completion of phases I and II of NATO's expansion to the comparatively stable north and west respectively. Neither phase was completed in time. By the final phases of NATO/ISAF's expansion to the south and south-east in 2006 (phases III and IV), the insurgency had become much more of a force to be reckoned with.

That Afghanistan had been viewed as a sideshow to Iraq in Washington[57] was evident in the limited number of coalition forces available to man "firebases" in provinces like Helmand and Uruzgan in the south-west prior to NATO's expansion south in 2006. Such limited forces on the ground could not prevent insurgents from moving beyond the remoter districts of the south-west and south-eastern provinces bordering Pakistan. As the insurgency spread across the south-west, south-east and to a lesser extent the east, its effects, which derived from internal as well as regional factors, increasingly hampered the ability of government and non-government actors to pursue development or the delivery of services. In the north, where the security situation was characterized by warlordism, comparative stability allowed the NGO and UN agencies to continue delivering services and development. However, it was a fragile stability, which depended on the consensus of the de facto powerful; a consensus that could be withdrawn at any time and without warning should circumstances change.[58]

DISPARATE PRT APPROACHES

The phased expansion of NATO starting in October 2003 in the north and ending in September 2006 in the east gradually brought all PRTs under NATO's command. For both Afghanistan and NATO, a tremendous amount was at stake. NATO's future viability in the post-Cold War world was now hostage to its fortunes in Afghanistan, while Afghanistan was urgently in need of course correction if growing public perceptions, inside and outside the country, that the state-building project was drifting towards the rocks were to be arrested. As mentioned, NATO's takeover of PRTs had led to increasingly disparate PRT approaches due to the plethora of national leads, differing agendas, and respective lists of national caveats.[59] The latter limited the types of PRT engagement and/or use of PRT resources. In addition, ISAF's chain of command only covered the PRTs' military components. The embedded civilian development and political advisers, considered vital by the military and donors to achieving the overall effect of expanding the Afghan government's authority and ensuring alignment with the Afghan National Development Strategy, reported back to their embassies and capitals.

The inability of NATO member states to agree on the roles and objectives of PRTs was reflected in the continued absence of a detailed PRT mandate, despite PRTs being at the leading edge of NATO's effort in Afghanistan. The question of overcoming the diversity of PRT approaches that derived from the lack of a detailed mandate, formerly a relatively marginalized NGO concern, now moved higher up the international agenda. A series of NATO conferences hosted by NATO headquarters and NATO member states during the course of 2005[60] focused on indirect ways to introduce greater coherence into the civil-military approach and improve coordination between PRTs and other actors. The concept of "Concerted Planning and Action" was promoted by the Danes, while NATO's "Comprehensive Approach" was reaffirmed at the 2006 Riga Summit as official policy.[61]

ISAF IX (May 2006–January 2007) devoted considerable resources to attempts to improve PRT coherence indirectly. Training courses based on field experience were held regularly both in Kabul and in NATO bases overseas for incoming PRT personnel. A PRT Handbook was developed and updated in consultation with UNAMA, UN agencies, and NGOs. Best practice was highlighted throughout and informed the PRT conferences for PRT commanders regularly held in Kabul. The mechanisms governing PRTs, the PRT Executive Steering Committee and the PRT Working Group, were reinvigorated and a number of PRT Executive Steering Committee "Policy Notes" were developed. These addressed critical areas where PRTs could make important contributions such as PRT support for provincial Disaster Management Teams[62] and for the Disbandment of Illegally Armed Groups (DIAG).

It was not clear what impact, if any, these policy notes actually had in the field where PRT personnel with limited resources had to cope with ever more visitors and report on their engagement in an increasing number of political processes. The relationship between PRTs and ISAF HQ began to bear some comparison with the problems that had historically surrounded the weak relations between Kabul and the periphery. In other words, the field could ignore instructions from headquarters, should it so choose. Or instructions from headquarters might be viewed in the field as irrelevant to realities as assessed on the ground and only ticked off in reports back to headquarters or national capitals. An underlying purpose of ISAF's efforts to improve PRT coherence was to heighten "situational awareness" prior to deployment, particularly with reference to other development actors in the field. Pre-deployment training also offset the loss of lessons learned during brief military rotations. However, the failure to develop an effective Afghan cadre in the PRTs, the lack of which also exacerbated the impact of rapid military rotations, was not addressed. But beyond tactical considerations, efforts to improve the alignment of PRT activities with the government's Afghan National Development Strategy brought the possibility of a workable exit strategy, in theory, closer.

The involvement of more and more nations in PRTs saw a "Balkanization" of the aid effort. Troop-contributing nations' development funding was increasingly directed towards the provinces in which respective nations' PRTs were located. Some European NGOs came under pressure from some European capitals to relocate programmes to the same province as their national PRT. NGOs often rely on government funding and are vulnerable in this regard.

Afghan Perspectives

There has been surprisingly little research conducted on Afghan perspectives of PRTs. However, one civil society organization that engaged in civic education in the run up to the presidential elections in 2004 found a degree of mistrust, as was confidentially noted by a civic education partner in Kunduz. "Government people introduce the projects to the PRTs and they don't provide the right guidance. They employ corrupt people." Afghan journalists and aid workers in 2005 who traveled extensively in the country confirmed that Afghans saw the PRTs as being tarred by the brush of an officialdom mainly seen as corrupt or ineffective. "How can a PRT make a corrupt official legitimate?" I was asked by a young Afghan journalist in 2005. The answer was that aside from recommending the removal of the official in question, further action was outside the remit of any PRT.

The civil society initiative on voter education reached over eight million Afghans in the run up to the parliamentary elections. Civic education processes were conducted through a network of fifteen local organizations in nearly all thirty-four provinces. During the parliamentary elections, over 1,500 male and female civic educators nation-wide were employed. The UN and USAID suggested that this voter education network kept in touch and exchanged information with PRTs to increase their security. All the Afghan civil society organizations involved declined this offer. They were wary of what was seen as another military structure, amongst many in Afghanistan, with an unclear purpose and mandate, and that association with PRTs, especially in the problematic south, would increase their security risk.

By 2005, the continued targeting of NGO staff by forces opposed to the government had rendered the concept of humanitarian space far more relevant to Afghan NGO staff. The Afghan director of the Kandahar office of an international NGO was adamant that any foreign military presence, including PRTs, arriving in an area where his staff was working posed an unacceptable risk. In such circumstances, he would order his NGO staff to leave the area. By May 2006 the director of an Afghan NGO umbrella organization based in Kandahar informed me that he avoided any meetings that included representatives of international organizations, including the UN. Just to attend meetings of organizations seen as supporting the government had become too dangerous, as meetings were being watched. By 2007, the risk to NGO staff in being directly associated with government development programmes was of increasing concern to NGO country directors.

The PRTs provided an important means of overcoming the information deficit, if they got out and about.[63] But they had always been associated by Afghans with intelligence gathering in the south. A PRT might visit a community to assess needs in the morning. The next day the same community might be subjected to coalition operations under Operation Enduring Freedom which was mandated to fight the war on terror. As forces opposed to the government strengthened and kinetic operations increased, confusion over the purposes of PRTs mounted.[64]

Though the PRTs insisted that Afghans knew the difference between coalition forces and the PRTs, they were wearing the same uniform as coalition forces in the east (and in the south until 2006). Also, Special Forces could operate out of uniform, making it impossible to distinguish between them and PRT civilian advisers. As four humvees carrying sixteen US soldiers usually accompanied State Department officials embedded in PRTs to meetings with community elders, this also affected Afghan perceptions. Moreover, in areas where the insurgency was underway, Special Forces operated out of PRT compounds, and detainees were brought to PRT compounds for interrogation or could be sent on to detention facilities in Bagram, the main US military base.[65]

Until 2006, the overall picture gained from personal and professional exchanges with civil society and NGO interlocutors with extensive networks at the grass roots remained unchanged. They consistently reported that the Taliban were seen as the least of Afghanistan's problems. The growing view that support for the insurgency was primarily driven by poor governance, continued impunity, and corruption (amongst other factors) was recognized by international policy makers. However, the ongoing failure to get an integrated approach across the different pillars of security reform processes, which were led by different G8 nations,[66] the weak outcomes of political reform processes from the civil service to the police, and the failure of the central government to provide sufficient support to the provinces, added up to a situation in which the PRTs were seen as de facto primary actors, usefully situated country-wide. Though able to act, this was mainly in ways that supported the authorities who, in principle, "owned" the state building process.

In some instances, local people challenged the status quo. Such initiatives tended to be led by ad hoc groupings of respected, and therefore influential, members of Afghan communities, politically ranged from leftists to conservatives. In May 2005 in northern Takhar, a protest against a commander led by teachers, mullahs, and medics mobilized several hundred people. The commander's militia promptly started beating people up, which precipitated a response from the PRT. UNAMA considered that the Afghans had taken a considered risk to draw the PRT in. However, this only paid off in the short term. A few months later, a new commander of the same PRT did not follow in his predecessor's footprints. A carefully prepared plan to disarm a local commander led by UNAMA with strong local support came to nothing when the PRT in question pulled out at the last minute. The PRT's actions in this case also jeopardized the start of the DIAG process in the region.[67]

The main effort of the international community had been focused initially on ensuring the security of the state. This was exemplified by the presence of ISAF forces in Kabul from early 2002 in the interests of preventing a coup. But as the threat of a coup diminished over time, direct steps to improve the worsening human security of the Afghan people do not appear to have been at the forefront of military planning. Instead, NATO stated its broad intent to establish security to enable the government and other development actors to access insecure areas of the country.

The difficulties NATO has faced in increasing troop levels to its mission to Afghanistan have been well documented by the media, and senior NATO (civilian and military) representatives have gone on record with their concerns. Such shortcomings have reduced ISAF's options, but the failure to be in a position to take meaningful steps to provide an enabling environment at local levels that would have strengthened civil society has been a missed opportunity at a number of levels. Afghans concluded that the PRTs were largely irrelevant in terms of their human security. But most significantly the opportunity that consistent actions, directed at providing an enabling environment for people, would have represented in establishing the moral intent of the international presence in Afghanistan, has been lost.

An overall loss of hope and trust that the international intervention can bring about a sustainable stability has developed alongside the "mafia-ization" of the state on the one hand and the increased strength of anti-government forces on the other. Afghan perceptions of the government have become increasingly negative owing to its skyrocketing corruption, its ineptitude, and perhaps most of all, its weakness. The terror tactics of the Taliban have had the desired effect, and people are much more afraid. Afghan employees of international organizations in provinces surrounding Kabul have moved their families (who could be targeted because of their work) to the relative safety of Kabul. A Pashtun who traveled regularly to the south over the last six years told me he would not be returning; "The killers are back," he said simply.

CONCLUSION

Afghanistan needed a heavy footprint at the outset and a light one as the country gradually stabilized. Instead, the reverse occurred. The decision to confine ISAF to Kabul at the outset of the Bonn Process was a turning point that weakened Afghan confidence in the nature of the international commitment. The objectives of the US-led war on terror, which is the leading priority of the US government, outweighed state-building objectives at critical junctures, particularly in terms of establishing the central government's more comprehensive control over the means of violence prior to the 2004 and 2005 Afghan elections. The priority of keeping the Bonn Process on track, which led the international effort from 2002–05, rendered security sector reform, *the* prerequisite for sustainable stability, a secondary affair. As a result, political structures and processes were established that outstripped licit economic development or improvements to the human security of the Afghan people. Consequently, the legitimization crisis surrounding the Afghan government has continued unabated. The PRT plan was predicated on the need for an enabling environment for reconstruction and development, which in turn, would improve the security environment and expand the government's legitimacy. the This formula, in the context of Afghanistan, amounted to a hope based on an assumption. The key question of how the security needs of the Afghan people would be protected was only addressed by the PRT concept in the broadest terms.

The weak outcomes of police reform closely linked to the failure to implement thorough reforms to the Ministry of Interior have undermined the military gains made by NATO, the coalition, and the Afghan National Army in the south and south-east. All actors are well aware that military operations have a short time span before they become counterproductive, as the increasing debate over the issue of civilian casualties has shown both inside Afghanistan and in European capitals. But the failure of Afghan security forces to hold ground cleared is only part of the equation. A police force capable of winning the trust and confidence of the Afghan people is another.

The expansion of PRT numbers and funding has not had a significant impact on the interlinked political and security crises in Afghanistan, which continue to move in a downward trend. The contributions of PRTs to the development needs of Afghanistan, which require a carefully nuanced approach over time and effective oversight, are coming under increasing scrutiny. During the period in which PRT numbers have increased throughout the country, security conditions, particularly in the south-west and south-east, have deteriorated, and national and international assistance actors have increasingly lost access to the rural hinterland. The assumption that reconstruction and development would buy stability in Afghanistan created a chicken and egg situation, one in which the "egg" of improvements to human security has so far not been laid.

In many respects, the PRTs may have proved more relevant to the needs of the international community by allowing the public promotion of good news over bad, than to the stabilization of the country. Internally, the positive spinning of information up the chain of command in response to the requirement for good news was also a factor distancing planners from facts on the ground, but one that was not unique to the military. This is not to discount the sustained efforts of PRT personnel in the field to get corrupt or ineffective officials replaced, but such efforts could only have limited effect if not matched by decisive will and political leadership in Kabul. Though PRTs have undoubtedly amounted to a way of sustaining international interest and directly involving nations in Afghanistan, other agendas have often propelled commitments. [68]

The disparate nature of PRT approaches, which largely derived from the absence of a detailed mandate, indicated the greater void caused by the lack of a unified, overall strategy for Afghanistan, particularly in the critical area of security sector reform. The main success of reform in this sector has been the development of a new Afghan army from scratch, which nevertheless is not yet trusted to operate independently (beyond battalion level) from its international mentors.

Even if a PRT mandate had been agreed to, it would have required the active commitment of troop-contributing nations for its implementation. The inability of NATO member states to subjugate national agendas to the interests of forging a unified policy in Afghanistan does not lend confidence in this regard. The locating of PRTs in twenty-five provinces appeared to offer NATO/ISAF countrywide reach. But the latter was undermined by the diversity of PRT approaches, the long list of national caveats which constrained the use of PRT assets, the extenuated chain of command, and the fact that limited manpower was overwhelmed by the size of the area under their watch. The fact that civilian elements embedded in PRTs remained outside NATO/ISAF's chain of command

and reported to national capitals further added to the difficulties ISAF confronted in attempts to introduce greater coherence to the effect of PRTs on the ground.

PRTs were also linked from the outset to the shoring up of the Bonn Process. Perhaps it is not surprising that, following the completion of the political benchmarks that punctuated the Bonn Process in swift succession from 2002 to 2005 and in the face of a growing insurgency, a more critical look is being directed towards the output of PRTs. The presence of PRTs also served to distract attention within and beyond Afghanistan from the limited progress being made in improving governance at provincial and district levels. Real progress in this critical area depended on the wider political context that was beyond the capacity of PRTs to alter. The political constraints therein on state building and stabilization processes were either avoided or lost out to political accommodations based on decisions governed by *realpolitik* that were externally, as well as internally, driven.

Despite rhetoric to the contrary, the international community has mainly responded to symptoms and has appeared either unable or unwilling to address underlying causes. Unless that situation changes, Afghanistan will continue to move in directions contrary to the democratic course intended by the architects of the Bonn Agreement and voted for by the Afghan people. Given this extremely worrying context, the degree of international attention and debate over the utility of the civil-military relationship in Afghanistan can be compared to rearranging the deckchairs on the Titanic.

NOTES

Barbara J. Stapleton is Deputy to the Office of the EU Special Representative for Afghanistan. This paper is written in her personal capacity.

1. Barbara J. Stapleton, "BAAG Briefing Paper on the Development of Joint Regional Teams," Jan. 2003, <www.baag.org.uk/publications/reports.htm>.
2. The political transition is commonly referred to as the Bonn Agreement or Bonn Process, which was decided at an international conference in the German city of Bonn in December 2001.
3. *The U.S. Army Marine Corps Counterinsurgency Field Manual, U.S. Army Field Manual* No. 3–24, Marine Corps Warfighting Publication No. 3-33.5, Chicago/London: University of Chicago Press, 2007, 53–77.
4. Mark Duffield, *Global Governance and the New Wars*, (London/New York: Zed Books, 2001), 161.

5. This was also a significant constraint for the central government, whose ranks were filled with many individuals who were returning technocrats who had grown up abroad.
6. Gilles Dorronsoro, *Revolution Unending* (London: Hurst & Company, 2005), 354.
7. Leon B. Poullada, *Reform and Rebellion in Afghanistan, 1919–1929: King Amanullah's Failure to Modernise a Tribal Society* (Ithaca/London: Cornell University Press, 1973), 269–70; Bijan Omrani, "Afghanistan and the Search for Unity," *The Royal Society for Asian Affairs*, vol. XXXVIII, no. 11, July 2007.
8. UNDP, *Afghanistan National Human Development Report 2004*, 165.
9. The security situation has militated against the conduct of field research by social anthropologists, and contemporary analysis of power relations at community levels remains limited.
10. Antonio Giustozzi, "Respectable Warlords? The Politics of Statebuilding in Post-Taleban Afghanistan," Crisis States Programme, Working paper no. 33, Series 1, London School of Economics, Sept. 2003, <www.crisisstates.com/publications/phase1htm>; Niamatullah Nojumi, *The Rise of the Taliban in Afghanistan* (New York: Palgrave, 2002).
11. Dorronsoro, *Revolution Unending*, 355.
12. William Maley, *The Afghan Wars* (New York: Palgrave Macmillan, 2002).
13. William Maley, *Rescuing Afghanistan* (London: Hurst & Company, 2006), 32.
14. On the global Human Development Index, Afghanistan is ranked 174 out of 178 countries. The Human Poverty Index views the country as one of the worst in the world. "Afghanistan Human Development Report 2007," Centre for Policy and Human Development, Kabul University, 27 Sept., emphasizes the links between human development and the rule of law.
15. Ray Jennings, "The Road Ahead, Lessons in Nation Building from Japan, Germany and Afghanistan for Postwar Iraq," Washington DC: United States Institute of Peace Press, 2003, <www.usip.org/pubs/index.html>.
16. Thorough political reform of the Ministry of Interior, on which police reform depends, is still pending.
17. A civil society expert cited one Afghan businessman as stating that "he loved his country but he loved his money more." By 2006, advertisements on Afghan TV stations regularly featured property for sale in Dubai as those profiting from the black economy increasingly invested abroad.
18. Author's interview in Kabul, July 2003, with Professor Kenji Izesaki, Japan's Special Representative on DDR, 2003–04.
19. Reliance by NATO on US airlift capacity in Afghanistan was still apparent in the run up to the 2005 parliamentary elections. On 25 Apr., the NATO Secretary General stated that any increase in NATO troops to boost security for the elections would depend on the availability of US airlift.
20. Richard A. Clarke, *Against All Enemies*, (New York: Free Press, 2004), 241.

21. Foreign aid workers had assumed that PRTs would provide support in extremis, but in cases of civil disturbances in Faizabad in the north-east, the PRT on both occasions withdrew into its compound.

22. The UN-facilitated evaluation of the initial three PRTs took place in Kabul in May 2003.

23. The extent of the problems confronted by the international community in rebuilding the Afghan state was becoming clearer. Initial assessments conducted prior to the first international donors conference in Tokyo, Jan. 2003, were conducted very superficially, as there was little time available.

24. Statement of Nancy Lindborg, Executive Vice-President, Mercy Corps, Senate Foreign Relations Committee hearing on: "Afghanistan: In Pursuit of Security and Democracy," 23 Oct. 2003.

25. Stapleton, *BAAG*, 27.

26. Author's interview with UNAMA official, Dec. 2004, during a period when UNAMA, with NGO support, had failed to get specific guidelines for the civil-military relationship in Afghanistan on to the agenda of the PRT Executive Steering Committee.

27. From 2003 onwards, a shift in the US government's position on ISAF's expansion occurred due to the need to get more non-US boots on the ground in Afghanistan as the situation in Iraq took up increasing resources.

28. The US shift in focus was reflected in guidelines ("Principles Guiding PRT Working Relations with UNAMA, NGOs and Local Government") by Ambassador Bill Taylor's office at the US embassy in 2003.

29. The commanders in question were the Uzbek general, Dostum (Junbesh), and the Tajik general, Atta (Jamiat); the latter became governor of Balkh Province.

30. Stapleton, *BAAG*, 19.

31. In early 2004, senior UNAMA representatives linked the increased engagement in state building by the US with the need for an exit strategy due to increasing security demands in Iraq. However, the massive new US embassy then under construction and commitment of substantial assets to the main US bases in Bagram and Kandahar indicated longer term plans.

32. Andrew Wilder, "Afghan Elections: The Great Gamble," *Afghan Research and Evaluation Unit* (Kabul, Nov. 2003).

33. QIP's figures for the Helmand PRT in 2006/07 amounted to US$12 million, and for 2007/08, US$18 million, according to a DfID representative.

34. By 2006/07, US PRT commanders and the US Regional Command were funded from a central fund of US$100 million that was disbursed by Task Force 82 as fast as the commanders could spend it, according to a development expert working with the British government's Department for International Development.

35. Over 2,500 NGOs were registered with the Afghan government by 2005, the majority of them Afghan. Many of these were "brief-case NGOs," consisting of one person with a bank account. A relatively small number of national

and international NGOs that met internationally recognized professional standards were registered with ACBAR, the umbrella NGO organization.

36. Robert M. Perito, "The U.S. Experience with Provincial Reconstruction Teams in Afghanistan: Lessons Identified," United States Institute of Peace, Special Report 152, Oct. 2005.
37. An exception was the length of tour by US forces, which by 2007 had extended to 14 months.
38. Mazar-e-Sharif (UK in July) in Bamyan (New Zealand in September) and in Kunduz (Germany in October).
39. The possibility of antagonizing local populations by direct involvement of NATO/ISAF forces in eradication of poppy crops has continued to be central to NATO policy.
40. "Aid Effectiveness in Afghanistan: At a Crossroads," *ACBAR Briefing Paper,* Nov. 2006.
41. Jim Hoagland, "The Key to Afghanistan: More Time," *Washington Post,* 24 Sept. 2006.
42. Twenty-eight aid workers were killed in 2004 and thirty-one in 2005. By the first half of 2006, this figure had already been exceeded (Figures: ACBAR).
43. The murder of four international staff and one national staff of Medecins sans Frontieres in Badghis Province in 2004 was later attributed to a disgruntled district chief of police who was due to be removed from his post. The car bomb attack against UNAMA's regional office in Kandahar in the same year was also believed by the UN to be linked to local politics rather than to insurgent attack.
44. The leader of the Zadran tribes, Jalaluddin Haqqani, is based in Pakistan and is closely linked to the Taliban.
45. According to PRT sources, up to fifteen suicide bombers looking for targets could be found in the provincial capital of Helmand at any one time in mid–2007.
46. Author's interview, PRT development adviser, 22 Aug. 2007.
47. Pamela Constable, "A NATO Bid to Regain Afghans' Trust," *Washington Post*, 27 Nov. 2006.
48. David Rohde, "Afghan Forces Suffer Setbacks as Taliban Adapt," *International Herald Tribune*, 1 Sept. 2007.
49. Author's interview with Kandahar-based Afghan researcher, 5 Sept. 2007.
50. *ACBAR Briefing Paper,* 2006, 2.
51. Sarah Lister, "Caught in Confusion: Local Governance Structures in Afghanistan," *AREU Briefing Paper,* Mar. 2005.
52. The PRT Working Group is attended by government, donor, coalition, ISAF, and UN representatives.
53. Sarah Lister and Hamish Nixon, "Provincial Governance Structure in Afghanistan: From Confusion to Vision?" *AREU Briefing Paper,* May 2006.

54. *Counterinsurgency Field Manual*, 57.
55. World Bank, "Service Delivery and Governance at the Sub-National Level in Afghanistan," July 2007, 46.
56. Michael R. Gordon, "NATO Flirts with Failure in Afghanistan," *International Herald Tribune*, 21 May 2004.
57. David Rohde and David E. Sanger, "How a 'Good War' in Afghanistan Went Bad," *New York Times*, 12 Aug. 2007.
58. The PRT in Mazar e Sharif had regular meetings with the prominent commanders in 2003 and was able to mitigate tensions in this way. There were occasions, however, when commanders would respond with force to events and with no prior warning to the PRT.
59. The list was an extensive one, according to a former ISAF commander, filling over eight pages of small print.
60. The author attended and spoke at four NATO hosted or jointly hosted conferences on civil-military coherence in 2004–05.
61. General Ray Henault, "Reviewing Riga," *NATO Review*, Spring 2007.
62. Military resources, especially air resources, were of crucial importance for emergency response in humanitarian emergencies caused by the natural disasters Afghanistan is prone to.
63. The extent to which PRTs proactively conducted patrols/outreach within respective areas of operation varied widely. Constraints were derived from instructions from capitals as well as security conditions on the ground.
64. Confusion over the purpose of the international military presence per se was widespread by 2007 and had been detectable in Kandahar from 2004. Conspiracy theories revolving around US or CIA backing for the neo-Taliban were standard by 2005–06. In a July 2007 interview with an Afghan contractor from Ghazni, a province in the south-east bordering Kabul, I was told that people there were convinced that the Taliban were receiving regular payments from coalition forces.
65. Author's interview with UNAMA political analyst, Aug. 2007.
66. Judicial reform was led by Italy, counter-narcotics by the UK, the Afghan army by the US, DDR/DIAG by Japan, and police reform by Germany.
67. Barbara Stapleton, "Civil Society Perspectives on the Role of PRTs," PRT "Best Practices" Conference, NATO Headquarters, 28–29 Nov. 2005.
68. For former Eastern European nations, the commitment to Afghanistan is driven by a desire to be on board NATO; for Japan, as debates in the Diet have illustrated, the commitment to OEF operations is informed by Japan's close relationship to to US interests.

The Civil-Military Effort in Afghanistan: A Strategic Perspective

Colonel M.D. (Mike) Capstick
(Canadian Forces, Retired)

ABSTRACT

Since the final objectives of the Bonn Process were met in the Fall of 2005, the security situation in the south of Afghanistan has deteriorated to the point that substantive economic development has been retarded. The more serious consequences of this situation include an erosion of public confidence in the elected government's ability to consolidate peace and stability, a burgeoning poppy industry, and an increase in generalized lawlessness and "war-lordism". Internationally, the persistence of the insurgency has caused any number of Western leaders to question the continued viability of their national commitments to the future of Afghanistan.

This situation is the result of a number of serious strategic errors – military and civilian. This paper will describe these and will use the Afghan Compact as the framework to suggest a major reorientation of the international effort so that it accords with this vital joint Afghan/international strategic vision. It will also suggest some measures to improve coordination among all international and Afghan actors to ensure the future of the Afghan people.

MISSED STRATEGIC OPPORTUNITIES

The international effort to bring stability and security to Afghanistan has been characterized by a growing list of missed strategic opportunities – both on the part of international military forces and the development community.

Driven by "transformational imperatives," the United States (US) military strategy to depose the Taliban regime depended on a unique combination of airpower, Special Forces, and local militias. However, the unintended, but totally foreseeable, consequence of the American reluctance to deploy major ground forces was that the power and prestige of some problematic warlords and commanders was reinforced. This was then exacerbated by American insistence that the UN-mandated International Security Assistance Force (ISAF) limit operations to Kabul.

Particulars of Original Publication:
Reprinted with permission of the *Journal of Military and Strategic Studies* (Fall, 2007). Available online from <http://www.jmss.org/2007/2007fall/

The ostensible reason for this was to allow US (Operation Enduring Freedom [OEF]) forces to pursue counter-terrorist operations in the remainder of the country. This "dual" chain of command persisted in violation of well established military principles and common sense until late 2006, when NATO assumed command of operations throughout the entire country. Even now, Special Operations and security transition activities remain outside the NATO chain of command.

Since 2001 US strategy has essentially been an "economy of force" effort. The number of "boots on the ground" is still not sufficient to establish the level of security necessary to permit substantive development to begin, and the tactics employed have failed to provide the population with a basic level of security. Further, the consequent security vacuum provided many warlords the opportunity to consolidate their regional power and to tighten their grip on poppy cultivation and other criminal enterprises.[1]

From the military perspective, much of this lack of coherence can be attributed to one basic but critical mistake – the collective failure of American and NATO leaders to understand the true nature of conflict in failed and failing states. This failure led to the application of military force using concepts, doctrine, tactics, and equipment optimized for "state-on-state" conflicts characterized by clashes between similarly organized military forces but not well-adapted to the realities of warfare waged by non-state actors in failed and failing states.[2] As retired British General Rupert Smith explains, "war among the people" [3] is, in essence, an effort by weaker adversaries (usually, but not always, non-state actors) to use tactics and weapons intended to minimize the advantages that a high-tech, industrial-age army brings to the battle. These adversaries avoid confrontations that could result in a decisive defeat; they adopt guerilla and terror tactics and achieve their *force protection* by blending into the population. In short, they fight "among the people". This, in turn, forces industrial-age military forces to do the same, using structures, munitions, and equipment optimized for a clash of armies. Smith concludes that this limits the utility of current Western armed forces in this kind of conflict and forces adaptation while engaged in the fight, and that the consequences are evident in Afghanistan.

The civilian effort has been plagued by a similar lack of strategic vision, an incoherent approach, and a major failure with respect to the development of the instruments of good governance. Like the military effort, international support of the Afghan government, in terms of both governance and economic development, has been dominated by an economy of force attitude and a lack of consistent strategic vision. In a 2005 article in the *World Policy Journal,* Carl Robichaud of the Century Foundation stated that "the international community has pursued a minimalist approach, both in troop commitments and reconstruction funding."[4] A recent *New York Times* critique of the Afghan mission is even more scathing in its assessment of the American effort, as is evident in the following quote:

> When it came to reconstruction, big goals were announced, big projects identified. Yet in the year Mr. Bush promised a "Marshall Plan" for Afghanistan, the country received less assistance per capita than did post-conflict Bosnia and Kosovo, or even desperately poor Haiti, according to a RAND Corporation study.[5]

At its core, this failure to translate victory in the battle against the Taliban regime into strategic victory in the war for the future of Afghanistan is the end product of international incoherence and a failure to understand that winning battles is simply not enough to ensure strategic success. Despite the overwhelming historical evidence that military force alone cannot defeat an insurgency or stabilize a failed state, the international community's efforts in Kabul have been characterized by an apparent lack of strategic vision and strategic level coordination of the civil-military effort. Although the Bonn Process succeeded in its aim of establishing the building blocks of statehood, there was no agreed international strategy that linked the essential security, governance, and development aspects of nation building until the Afghanistan Compact[6] was approved at the London Conference in February 2006. Even after the promulgation of the Compact, implementation efforts have suffered from the same strategic incoherence that has been so evident throughout the Afghan mission.[7]

Establishing effective civil-military coordination measures to ensure that security, governance, and development efforts are synchronized is only the essential first step in achieving coherence. International and Afghan efforts within each of these realms must also be fully integrated. In short, "unity of effort" must be the master principle of the Afghan mission and become part of the operating culture of every single entity involved.

THE MILITARY CONCEPT

The American-led attack against the Taliban regime was initially characterized as a validation of the Pentagon's transformational vision of warfare. High technology precision weapons systems, satellite communications, and sophisticated command and control networks allowed the American military to defeat the Taliban regime without deploying large numbers of ground troops.

THE THREE BLOCK WAR CONCEPT

The term "Three Block War" was coined by General Charles C. Krulak, the 31st Commandant of the United States Marine Corps. He first used it in a speech to the National Press Club in Washington in December

1997 and never formally developed the concept in any rigorous fashion. General Krulak was among the most colourful Marine officers of his generation; he is also credited with developing the phrase "Strategic Corporal" to capture the intellectual and ethical demands that even the most junior levels of leadership face in the "post-modern" battlespace. Krulak described the Three Block War (3BW) as follows:

> Our enemies will not allow us to fight the Son of Desert Storm, but will try to draw us into the stepchild of Chechnya. In one moment in time, our service members will be feeding and clothing displaced refugees, providing humanitarian assistance. In the next moment, they will be holding two warring tribes apart – conducting peacekeeping operations – and finally they will be fighting a highly lethal mid-intensity battle – all on the same day, all within three city blocks. It will be what we call the "three block war". In this environment, conventional doctrine and organizations may mean very little. It is an environment born of change.[8]

The Three Block War metaphor seized the imagination of military analysts and intellectuals, and like most metaphors, has been abused ever since. It is important to place Krulak's imagery in the context of the times. In 1997 the US military establishment was still basking in the glow of the hundred hours of ground combat that ended in victory in Operation Desert Storm. The "Revolution in Military Affairs", precision weapons, information superiority, and concepts like network-centric warfare and rapid decisive operations dominated American military thinking. The Marine Corps was the only service to resist this latest, high-tech interpretation of the attritional "American Way of War". Officers like Krulak and General Anthony Zinni clearly understood that war is an essentially human event and that people – soldiers, political leaders, the affected population, and the citizenry of our own nations – are far more important than technology as determinants of victory. Before most other military leaders and analysts, they also understood that the dominance of state-on-state warfare was in decline. In the aftermath of the Cold War, there was no peer competitor with sufficient military power to challenge the US in any conventional military sense. They understood that, in the absence of direct military threats to the survival of Western states, most future conflicts would be "wars of choice", and the enemy would have to adopt "asymmetrical" strategies and tactics in the face of the "overwhelming force" represented by American military power. In short, while the rest of the US military establishment was building on the legacy of Desert Storm, Krulak and the Marines saw the future in the streets of Grozny and Mogadishu, and they intended to be ready. The "three block war" idea was the shorthand that Krulak chose to use to describe this crucial, philosophical fault-line in American military thinking.

Like most shorthand, the term "three block war" cannot be expected to convey the full range of meaning intended by its author. The kind of conflict envisioned by General Krulak has been actualized in Afghanistan, Iraq, Lebanon, and in the persistent civil wars in parts of Africa. Current military theory refers to this type of conflict as "Fourth Generation Warfare" (4GW). One of the leading theorists in the field, retired Marine Colonel Thomas X. Hammes, describes 4GW as an "advanced insurgency" that uses "all available networks – political, economic, social, and military – to convince the enemy's decision makers that their strategic goals are either unachievable or too costly for the perceived benefit."[9] At its core, 4GW is strategic in nature as it targets the political will of its adversaries.

The 3BW imagery is, on the other hand, tactical. It uses the idea of three city blocks as the basis of the model and conjures up a graphic image of small tactical units engaged in combat, peacekeeping, and humanitarianism in a defined geographical area. The small unit image is further reinforced by Krulak's idea of the "strategic corporal" and the reality that small unit actions can have serious strategic consequences. In my view, the tactical imagery of the 3BW idea, although useful in the field, is one of the main conceptual obstacles leading to a lack of clarity at the strategic level.

It is clear that the Taliban are pursuing a fourth generation model of conflict in Afghanistan today, and it is equally clear that it has achieved a degree of strategic success in Kabul, in NATO capitals, and critically, in the minds of the people of troop contributing nations and Afghan citizens. Until now, the government of Afghanistan and NATO nations have often ceded the information advantage to the Taliban, and critically, they have failed to apply a strategic level, three block approach to the international effort. That said, the Afghanistan Compact provides an excellent strategic framework and a common language that must now be used to bring essential coherence to that effort. In short, its three pillars – security, governance, and economic and social development – are an appropriate conceptualization of the three blocks and offer a model for achieving a coherent and comprehensive Afghan mission.

In the remainder of this paper, I describe how the Compact reflects Krulak's 3BW shorthand at the strategic level. I also offer commentary concerning the reality of the insurgency and the problematic relationship between the military and the developmental aspects of "state building".

FOURTH GENERATION CONFLICT IN AFGHANISTAN

There has been intense political, media, and civil society group criticism of a perceived "imbalance" in Canadian strategy resulting from the military's involvement in combat operations in Kandahar. Some commentators have concluded that the mission has shifted away from state building and reconstruction towards a purely military, counter-insurgency role.[10] This conclusion can only result from a fundamentally flawed understanding of the insurgency itself. The Taliban-led terror campaign in the south and east is not a classical anti-colonial struggle, nor is it a simple battle of competing political ideologies. It is, instead, a battle between the forces of tradition and the advocates of modernity. The Taliban's objective is not mere territorial control or political power – it is control of the population and the re-establishment of the perverse theocracy that ruled until late 2001.[11] To that end, they have formed any number of alliances with drug lords and other criminals who profit from instability, and with international and national networks that share a common interest in ensuring that the rule of law remains weak. This amorphous coalition of groups is more than willing to use extreme violence to achieve their aims and has demonstrated time and again that development in the absence of basic security is futile. Finally, the fact that the insurgent coalition is a collection of groups with different motivations and interests and that much of its fighting power is provided by criminal gangs renders discussion of a "comprehensive peace process" moot. There is, in essence, no coherent insurgent leadership to negotiate with. There is no will on the part of the Taliban to negotiate, and legitimate governments simply cannot negotiate with armed criminal gangs – especially those that recognize no constraints on the use of violence against innocents.

The effect of this insurgency has been to retard both the establishment of proper governance structures and economic development in the southern provinces. To advocate "rebalancing" the mission effort in favour of the reconstruction effort while an active insurgency terrorizes the population is, at best, naïve. Defeating the insurgency is crucial to the overall success of the international effort in Afghanistan, regardless of the best intentions of those who would prefer to emphasize the developmental aspects of the mission.

The war in Afghanistan is, in effect, an "advanced insurgency" that meets the definitional standard of a fourth generation conflict. Two elections and extensive social science research provide ample evidence that the majority of Afghans categorically reject the insurgents' world view.[12] Recognizing the true nature of the insurgency, the UN Security Council endorsement of the Compact (including the security pillar) represents explicit approval of both the ongoing, American-led counter-insurgency operations and the ISAF transition concept.[13] Further, the Compact and Afghanistan's National Development Strategy explicitly address the social, political, and economic aspects of state building – an effort that must continue even while the security situation remains contested. In short, the international community, through the authority of the UN Security Council, has deliberately chosen to support the Afghan government and eliminated any question of neutrality or the traditional impartiality of UN peacekeeping with respect to the battle that continues to put the future of the country in jeopardy – a future that depends on a renewed international and Afghan effort to fully implement the strategy devised in London.

THE AFGHANISTAN COMPACT – THE STRATEGIC CIVIL–MILITARY CONCEPT

Almost three decades of insurgency, invasion, resistance, civil war, and ultimately, the American-led attack on the Taliban have left Afghanistan shattered. Despite this legacy of violence, the progress made since 2001 has been nothing short of spectacular. The Bonn Agreement[14] was, in essence, a political roadmap that allowed Afghans to take control of their own future. Even with the pressure of an ongoing insurgency, Afghanistan has promulgated a Constitution, held two very successful elections, opened Parliament, and restored a sense of normalcy in most of the country. Without a doubt, major problems persist – insurgency, opium, criminality, and most importantly, grinding and endemic poverty. Determined to overcome these obstacles, the government of Afghanistan, in partnership with the international community, is ready to take the next steps.

The "next steps" are mapped out in two crucial documents, The Afghanistan Compact and Afghanistan's National Development Strategy (ANDS),[15] both presented and approved at the recent London Conference. The Compact is essentially the political "deal" between Afghanistan and the world that strives to achieve the government's vision, stated here: "Our vision for the Islamic Republic of Afghanistan is to consolidate peace and stability through just, democratic processes and institutions, and to reduce poverty and achieve prosperity through broad based and equitable economic growth."[16]

This mutual commitment, endorsed by a unanimous resolution of the UN Security Council (1659–2006),[17] is best expressed in the Compact itself: "The Afghan government hereby commits itself to realizing this shared vision of the future; the international community, in turn, commits itself to provide resources and support to realize that vision."[18]

Both the Compact and ANDS are built around three "pillars". The first is security. This includes the international military contribution, defeating the insurgency, reform of the national army (ANA) and police (ANP), and the disbanding of illegal, armed groups. The second is governance, rule of law, and human rights. It encompasses reform of the machinery of government, re-vitalization of the civil service, justice reform, the fight against corruption and the poppy economy, and making the institutions of the state work for the people. The third pillar, economic and social development, is the real heart of the matter. It is under this pillar that the bulk of the reconstruction effort falls, and it is, in essence, the real objective of the ANDS. In addition to these pillars, both documents describe gender equity, counter-narcotics, regional co-operation, anti-corruption, and the environment as "cross-cutting themes", as these issues need to be dealt with in the context of all three pillars and at the societal level.[19]

The result of extensive consultation and a very concerted effort by both the international community and, most importantly, all elements of the government, the Compact, and ANDS received an extraordinary degree of consensus at the London Conference, as well as rare endorsement by a unanimous resolution of the UN Security Council. Together, these documents map the future of Afghanistan, and if properly implemented, they will establish the conditions necessary for Afghans to achieve their vision of a peaceful, just, democratic, stable, and prosperous Islamic state. At the strategic level, the Compact's pillars are, in essence, analogous to Krulak's three blocks at the tactical level. The security pillar covers the war-fighting and peacekeeping aspects of his concept. Peacekeeping is also part of the governance pillar, and the economic and social development pillar is an expanded version of the humanitarian aid block. This construct is a more appropriate conceptualization at the strategic level as it avoids both the tactical imagery and the spatial limitations of Krulak's original expression.

The parties to the Compact (the Government of the Islamic Republic of Afghanistan, the sixty-four nations that signed on in London, and the UN Security Council) clearly recognize the essentiality of coordinating their individual and collective efforts across all three pillars. Despite this recognition, implementation of the Compact is still problematic, and effective civil-military coordination in Kabul remains weak.[20]

There should be no doubt – the future of Afghanistan still hangs in the balance. Although a reasonable degree of security has been established in most of the country, there are areas in the south and east where the insurgency has prohibited major development projects. The institutions of the state are, for the most part, still weak, and the government is not yet capable of protecting the population. The outcome is by no means guaranteed. Achieving the vision will require a cohesive, coherent, and sustained international commitment to the Compact and ANDS. Canada and the Canadian Forces (CF) have a vital role to play in this commitment, as these documents represent a significant step forward in dealing with the fourth generation warriors currently terrorizing the people of Afghanistan and preventing development work in large parts of the country.

THE CANADIAN FORCES AND THE AFGHANISTAN COMPACT

GENERAL

The three pillars of the Afghanistan Compact suggest that there is a neat division of labour among the three lead Canadian government departments and agencies in Afghanistan with respect to their engagement. This is true in broad terms; the Department of Defence and the CF lead on security issues; the Department of Foreign Affairs and International Trade (DFAIT) leads on governance, rule of law, and human rights matters; and the Canadian International Development Agency (CIDA) is the focal point on the economic and social development front. Other departments and organizations also contribute. For example, the RCMP has officers in the Kandahar Provincial Reconstruction Team (PRT) and in the European Union Police Mission (EUPOL) Headquarters, and Corrections Canada supports the UN Assistance Mission Afghanistan (UNAMA). Despite this apparent clarity, the reality is rather more complex on the ground, and no Canadian government agency can operate strictly within one pillar or another. Although not necessarily obvious, the CF play a role in each of the three pillars as part of the cohesive, whole-of-government (WGA) approach that Canada is trying to apply as a means of achieving the best results on the ground. In turn, DFAIT and CIDA both have significant influence over, and are active in, the security sector. For example, the Ambassador and Head of Aid played key roles in the Disarmament, Demobilization and Reintegration (DDR) Program, a function of the security pillar.

The remainder of this section describes how the CF support each of the pillars of ANDS. This discussion will be through a CF lens, and it must be borne in mind that each of the other committed departments and agencies has a vital role to play in the efforts of the others.

The CF have been engaged in Afghanistan since the deployment of a combat unit to Kandahar in late 2001 as part of the American-led coalition (Operation Enduring Freedom/OEF). Although the number of troops has varied, the CF have made major contributions to both, mutually supporting multi-national forces in the country.[21] From 1 March until 1 November 2006, Canada assumed lead nation status in Regional Command (South). This region includes some of the most unstable provinces in the country, including Kandahar, Uruzugan, Helmand, Nimroz, and Kunduz. The commitment included the lead of the Multi-National Brigade Headquarters that exercises command over Canadian, British, American, Dutch, Romanian, and Australian units in the region. The Canadian commitment of around 2,500 troops currently includes an infantry battle group in Kandahar Province, the Kandahar PRT, and an Observer Mentor/Liaison Team (OMLT) embedded with ANA units in the province. This commitment was initially part of OEF, and as a result, became conflated in some quarters with the more unpopular aspects of US foreign policy. The Canadian mission (and Regional Command South) came under the command of the ISAF at the end of July 2006, and the Canadian-led command structure was instrumental in establishing the conditions for the successful transition from American to NATO command.

In late 2008, an Air Wing was added to provide the Task Force with tactical helicopter, air-lift, and unattended aerial vehicle (UAV) support.

In addition to the troops in RC(S) and Kandahar, the CF have a strong presence in Kabul. Canadian staff officers serve in both the ISAF and the coalition headquarters. Until 2008, the CF also contributed a fifteen-soldier training team that worked with ANA units to prepare them for deployment to the provinces. In addition, a small military/civilian team of planners (Strategic Advisory Team – Afghanistan/SAT-A) worked directly with Afghan government agencies to assist in the development of the strategic plans necessary to achieve the objectives of the Compact.

The Canadian Forces and the Security Pillar

It is clear that security is the non-negotiable prerequisite for the success of the Compact. In the absence of security, economic and social development is almost impossible. In addition, the insurgency presents a direct threat to the development of good governance structures and practices. As a result, the security pillar will continue to be the main focus of CF effort in Afghanistan for some time to come. Despite this emphasis, the Canadian Forces Campaign Plan for Afghanistan has three lines of operation that mirror the ANDS pillars.[22]

The battle group in Kandahar is organized and equipped to assist the provincial governor and the Afghan national army and police in their efforts to establish the legitimate government's "monopoly on the use of lethal force" in the province. The PRT, with military members, police and corrections officers, diplomats, and CIDA development specialists, is also heavily engaged in the security pillar. It "reinforces the authority of the Afghan government in and around Kandahar" and helps local authorities stabilize and rebuild the region. Its tasks are to monitor security, to promote the policies and priorities of the national government with local authorities, and to facilitate reform in the security sector."[23] An analysis of this mandate reveals that the PRT concept is illustrative of the reciprocity between security, governance, and development.

With the exception of the SAT-A in Kabul, almost every other CF member in the Kabul area is engaged with the security pillar. Canadian staff officers and troops at the ISAF and various coalitions headquarters are fully integrated in those organizations. The ANA training team and the OMLT are also clearly fully committed in this pillar as their work is "hands-on" tactical training of Afghan soldiers at the small unit level.

CF Support to Governance, the Rule of Law, and Human Rights

In this ANDS pillar, the most obvious examples of CF support are found in the PRT and the SAT-A. The PRT is, by its mandate, intended to "reinforce the authority of the Afghan government."[24] Although its focus has been on security because of the prevailing situation in the province, it has provided significant support to the Provincial Governor, the Afghan National Army, and the Afghan National Police, and by virtue of its development work, the line-ministries of the central government. This level of support will continue to grow as the intent is to co-locate part of the PRT headquarters in the governor's office.

The SAT-A had a direct role in the governance pillar as it has planning teams in direct support of a number of Afghan ministries including the Ministry of Rural Rehabilitation and Development ([MRRD] the main Afghan government agent for reconstruction outside of Kabul). The team has assisted in the development of the MRRD strategic plan. This included the strategy for the establishment of the comprehensive governance structure for development that extends from the village to the national level. In all cases, the team has formed working partnerships with international organizations such as the World Bank and the UN Development Program. Those bodies brought expertise in governance to the table while the SAT-A provided the skills to integrate their input and assist Afghan managers in the formulation of a coherent strategy. This work was a clear demonstration of the potential of military staff "skills transfer" to the civil sector in a post-conflict society that has had little time to develop viable public institutions and a culture of good governance. In August 2008 this team was re-deployed to Canada and a new civilian Canadian Governance Support Office (CGSO) replaced it to provide more focused technical assistance to specific ministries.

CF Support to the Economic and Social Development Pillar

Within the security envelope provided by the Battle Group in Kandahar Province, the PRT is focused on development and reconstruction. This includes support to alternative livelihood programmes, rural rehabilitation, and any number of public infrastructure projects. At the same time, The ISAF in general and the PRT in particular have renewed their emphasis on good governance. For example, the PRT provides direct support to the newly established Provincial Development Council and their district- and village-level equivalents. The unit is, by far, the best example of the whole-of-government concept at the tactical level as it includes senior diplomats, CIDA expertise (augmented by both the British Department for Foreign International Development and USAID), RCMP officers, and staff from Corrections Canada. It is the CIDA component, not the military, which plans and coordinates development activities, while the CF provide the basic security envelope and the essential support framework.

In addition to the Kandahar focus in the economic development pillar, the SAT-A in Kabul was directly involved with a planning team supporting the Afghan-led ANDS Working Group. Similar to the effort in the MRRD, it is the ANDS Working Group and international experts who provided the substantive and technical content, while the SAT-A applied military strategic planning methodology to ensure coherence, synchronization, and sequencing in the same way that it would for a military campaign.

Security and Development

The original articulation of the three block war (3BW) concept used tactical level language and imagery to make a very specific point about the changing character of "post-modern" conflict. Krulak was clearly concerned with the US military's intense focus on high-tech solutions and his aim was fairly simple – to restore the soldier and small unit to their rightful place on the battlefield. Given that the 3BW is most often discussed at the tactical level, the idea of soldiers delivering humanitarian aid is the most contested part of the concept. Much of this discussion is a "dialogue of the deaf" and is rooted in military and humanitarian values that were developed and practised in a far simpler world than the one we face today.

Recent operations in Afghanistan and Iraq have demonstrated that the 3BW concept is not as simple as Krulak's original articulation. Because there is, in any conflict, a clear moral duty for military forces to care for the population remaining in the combat zone to ensure that no further harm impacts innocent civilians, humanitarian aid delivered by military forces while fighting is still occurring must be, of military necessity, limited to the life-saving essentials demanded by the principle of the "duty of care". In reality, tactical combat units have very little capacity in this area and will remain focused on fighting the battle or maintaining a tenuous security situation. As soon as there is sufficient security in a specific area, traditional humanitarian organizations will commence operations and will, most often, provide the vast majority of aid using the values and principles espoused in the *Humanitarian Charter*, the *Code of Conduct*, and individual organizational guidance. Although this traditional construct carries risks, in that humanitarian organizations could find themselves providing medical care and food to the insurgents who are threatening the very same population that the organizations are trying to protect, military forces should still support this model as humanitarian NGOs are far more proficient and efficient in delivering this type of aid. Colonel Joseph Collins of the US Army War College has referred to this phase as "part one" of the "Humanitarian Assistance and Economic Development" block of the 3BW concept. In essence, it deals with the immediate humanitarian requirement to alleviate human suffering, and at least in my view, should be both impartial and independent as far as the security situation permits.[25]

Collins defines economic development, or political reconstruction, as part two of the block. Given the UNSC endorsement of the Afghanistan Compact, programmes and projects under the economic and social development pillar cannot be considered as impartial humanitarian aid. In short, the international community has chosen to support the government of Afghanistan and has endorsed a comprehensive plan that is intended to secure the future of the country. That said, in the Afghan case, it is in this stage that the military/development interface has become problematic. There are any number of contentious issues in this regard, and most are the result of a lack of role clarity and questions of professional jurisdiction – on both sides of the relationship.

Without a doubt, the PRT concept is a work in progress. Until 2006 NATO and PRTs operated with very different guidance. National caveats have detracted from the ability of ISAF HQ to coordinate PRT activities at the national level, and most importantly, a number of well-intentioned PRT commanders have initiated projects that do not reflect Afghan priorities and are of questionable sustainability. On the positive side, all of these issues have been recognized by the political/military chain of command in Afghanistan. In recent months the joint Afghan – International PRT Executive Steering Committee has been rejuvenated, ISAF HQ hosted the first NATOUS PRT Commanders Conference and has issued the first draft of a PRT handbook that is intended to provide more precise guidance. Crucially, The ISAF and the coalition have been making a strenuous effort to align PRT activities with the ANDS.

At the same time, there appear to be some unresolved issues in terms of the appropriate roles of official development agencies and NGOs. Clearly, official development agencies are arms of their parent governments, and their activities must support the national strategies and objectives of those governments. In other words, CIDA cannot and must not be viewed as either impartial or independent, as its activities form an integral part of Canada's overall strategy. However, most agencies, CIDA included, contract the delivery of programmes to private contractors or NGOs. This, in effect, makes the involved NGOs agents of the contracting government, and it cannot help but place their traditional impartiality in question. Only the NGO community can resolve the issues of principle that arise from this practice, but at a minimum, they cannot claim that their traditional impartiality pertains when they are acting on behalf of a national government or international organization.

These issues are often discussed at the tactical level. However, it is at the international and national levels that coherence and the coordination of military and development efforts is most crucial. The fourth generation adversary uses "all available networks – political, economic, social, and military...", and it is clear that the government of Afghanistan and the international community must seize the initiative and use the strategic framework provided by the Afghanistan Compact and Afghanistan's National Development Strategy to counter those networks.

STRATEGIC LEVEL CIVIL–MILITARY COORDINATION

In February 2007, after five years of almost continual Canadian involvement in Afghanistan, the government finally formed an Afghanistan Task Force in the Department of Foreign Affairs to oversee all aspects of the 3D mission. Under the leadership of an experienced diplomat, David Mulroney, the task force has the mandate, authority, and expertise to "develop the common narrative" and plans needed for success.[26] In 2008, this task force moved to the Privy Council Office and Mulroney was designated as Deputy Minister. This national level initiative promises to offer a significant improvement over the ad hoc coordination processes that were, often by default, led by the CF in the past.

Mulroney's team is tasked to develop a "single narrative, a single campaign plan for the three departments and all others who are engaged in Afghanistan." That narrative will be based on the Afghanistan Compact and will include those areas and sectors that are of particular interest to Canada such as justice and the rule of law. According to Mulroney, other nations such as the United Kingdom have instituted similar arrangements to coordinate their own national efforts in Afghanistan. Even though the establishment of these coordination arrangements is a fairly recent initiative, it is clear that strategic level coordination of the civil-military effort in Afghanistan (or in any intervention, for that matter) is essential in the face of any adversary that uses "all available networks – political, economic, social, and military – to convince the enemy's decision makers that their strategic goals are either unachievable or too costly for the perceived benefit."[27] That said, experience in Afghanistan provides ample evidence that security is the non-negotiable prerequisite for long-term economic development and the establishment of a governance structure that can deliver basic services to the population.

Although the Canadian national strategic-level, civil-military coordination structure (finally) seems to be a very important step in the right direction, a lack of coherence still characterizes the strategic situation in Kabul. In Afghanistan's Endangered Compact, the International Crisis Group described the feeble international effort to coordinate its activity across all three pillars of both the Afghanistan Compact and Afghanistan's National Development Strategy. A recent *Los Angeles Times* editorial claims that "(t)he setbacks in Afghanistan are fairly blamed on the Bush administration's decision to attempt nation building on the cheap. It then slashed aid in 2006 and diverted military and intelligence resources to the worsening situation in Iraq."[28] This lack of American strategic vision has been evident since the successful military campaign of 2001. Coupled with American dominance in Kabul, this lack of vision has been the main cause of continued international confusion in Kabul.[29]

If Afghanistan is to be "saved", the confusion in Kabul must be rectified – quickly. The International Crisis Group has made several recommendations pertaining to the Joint Coordination and Monitoring Board (co-chaired by the UN SRSG and an Afghan presidential appointee and charged with overseeing the Compact). Without debating the specifics, making this body effective must be an overriding international and Afghan priority in the short term. Accomplishing this will demand far greater co-operation among involved nations, the lead donors, and international agencies than has been evident thus far. On the civil side, only the UN can lead an effort of this magnitude. Simultaneously, NATO and the UN need to find a way to align the military and civil efforts at the strategic level. An inability to achieve this alignment can only lead to failure.

It is now time that the military chain of command be totally unified. Since November 2006 most operations have come under NATO command. However, the development of effective Afghan national army and police units are under a separate US command structure, as are Special Operations Forces. This situation is militarily untenable and must be fixed.

On the international civil-military front, it is long past time that the secretaries-general of the UN and NATO agree to appoint a high-profile and powerful joint special representative to coordinate all aspects of the effort. It is just as essential that the American administration recognize its state-building failures (magnified by its focus on Iraq) and actively support this special representative. At the same time, a joint Afghan/international civil-military structure needs to be put in place down to the provincial level. This structure would be responsible to the new special representative and the President of the Islamic Republic of Afghanistan and would have the authority to coordinate all aspects of Compact and ANDS implementation.[30]

Finally, the structural solutions described here will not, on their own, result in strategic coherence. All actors – military, diplomatic, and development – must subsume their individual national and bureaucratic objectives to the vision articulated in the Compact. The alternative is failure, and in the final analysis, the Afghan people will bear the costs of that failure.

Conclusion

Despite the pessimistic tone of much commentary, Afghanistan has seen some remarkable progress in the past four years. As part of the Bonn Process, the roadmap that established the basic political framework necessary for good governance, Afghans agreed upon a Constitution and held very successful presidential elections in October 2004 and parliamentary elections on 18 September 2005. These achievements should not be underestimated. Thirty years of conflict had not only destroyed the basic structures of the state and much of the physical infrastructure, it had also inflicted serious damage upon the social fabric of the country. This is the kind of damage that is almost impossible to see, but it is probably more significant than the kind that can be photographed and measured. Massive population movements have all but destroyed many of the traditional methods of social regulation and conflict resolution, and constant fighting has left the population with a collective case of psychological disruption. The success of the Bonn Process effectively signaled the collective commitment of the Afghan people to democratic processes over the power of the gun. In addition to this impressive political process, Afghans and the international community have established basic security in about three-quarters of the country. Hundreds of thousands of children, including girls, have returned to school. Clinics, roads, irrigation systems, and countless other development projects have been completed. Much of this work has been completed with little fanfare or media attention.

The Afghan state-building project is complex and complicated. The problems of criminality, corruption, poppy growing, poverty, and weak state institutions cannot be wished away. Instead, they can only be resolved by the concerted joint Afghan/international effort that was committed to at the London Conference. State building is a long and arduous process. Canada is one of thirty-six nations with military forces on the ground – even more countries are involved in development. Patience, resolve, and perseverance are essential if the people of Afghanistan are to see the results of the promises made in the past four years. We should have no illusions. Much remains to be done in Afghanistan, and the future of the country is by no means assured.

One of the major lessons of the Afghan experience is that economic development and good governance are essential elements of security and stability. Most military professionals have long recognized that military force alone is insufficient to defeat a determined insurgency, and that security without sustained development and good governance will inevitably be transitory. Although Canada's 3D strategy explicitly recognizes this reality, as do the strategies of several other nations, establishing security and accomplishing the vision of the Afghanistan Compact demands that all of these strategies be unified at the international level in Kabul.

NOTES

Some information in this article has been updated since it was originally prepared in 2007.

1. See Hy S. Rothstein, *Afghanistan and the Uncertain Future of Unconventional Warfare* (Annapolis, MD: Naval Institute Press, 2006), for a comprehensive discussion of the numerous strategic errors that have led to many of the problems faced by the Afghan government in 2005 and 2006.
2. General Sir Rupert Smith, *The Utility of Force: The Art of War in the Modern World* (London: Allan Lane, 2005), 394–98.
3. Smith uses this phrase throughout *The Utility of Force* to differentiate the kinds of conflict that have come to predominate in the post-Cold War era from more "traditional" conflicts such as WWII and Korea that inform the public's, military leaders', and politicians' views of war.
4. Carl Robichaud, "Remember Afghanistan? A Glass Half-Full on the Titanic," *World Policy Journal* (Spring 2006): 17.
5. David Rohde and David E. Sanger, "How a 'Good War' in Afghanistan Went Bad," *New York Times*, 12 Aug. 2007.
6. Islamic Republic of Afghanistan, *The Afghanistan Compact: A Strategy For Security, Governance, Economic Growth & Poverty Reduction* (Kabul: Islamic Republic of Afghanistan, 2006), <http://www.ands.gov.af/main.asp>.
7. See *Afghanistan's Endangered Compact*, International Crisis Group, Asia Briefing, No. 59, Brussels, 29 Jan. 2007, for a comprehensive and critical evaluation of Compact implementation.
8. Gen. Charles C. Krulak, USMC, "The Three Block War: Fighting in Urban Areas," *Vital Speeches of the Day* 64, no. 5 (New York: 15 Dec. 1997), 139–42.
9. Thomas X. Hammes, *The Sling and Stone: On War in the 21st Century* (St. Paul, MN: Zenith Press, 2004), 2.
10. For example, Linda McQuaig's polemic in the 12 Feb. 2006 edition of the *Toronto Star* is a particularly ill-informed critique of CF operations in Afghanistan. A more balanced view is offered in the Project Ploughshares Briefing #06/01. Entitled *Afghanistan: Counter-Insurgency by Other Means,* Ernie Rehger asks a number of valid questions that should be resolved by a careful reading of the Compact, ANDS, and CF statements. The UNSC endorsement in its resolution 1659 (2006) should satisfy those who question the legitimacy of the Canadian commitment.
11. Emily Hsu and Beth DeGrasse, *Afghan Insurgency Still a Potent Force,* USI Peace Briefing, Washington, Feb. 2006.
12. Charney Research, *ABC Poll: Life in Afghanistan*, 7 Dec. 2005, <http://www.charneyresearch.com/>; this poll found that 77 per cent of Afghans support the current government's "direction" for the future and that 88 per cent consider the American overthrow of the Taliban a "good thing". Similar

findings were made by the Center for Strategic and International Studies. See Frederick Barton, Bathsheba Crocker, and Morgan L. Courtney, *In the Balance: Measuring Progress in Afghanistan* (Washington: Center for Strategic and International Studies, 2005).

13. Islamic Republic of Afghanistan, *The Afghanistan Compact*, 6. The Compact is very specific in terms of the role of the government and all international forces in protecting the security and stability of the country. UNSC endorsement is a clear expression of support.

14. United Nations, *The Bonn Agreement*, <http://www.unama-afg.org/docs/_nonUN%20Docs/_Internation-Conferences&Forums/Bonn-Talks/bonn.htm>.

15. Both are available at <http://www.ands.gov.af/main.asp>.

16. Islamic Republic of Afghanistan, *Afghanistan National Development Strategy, Summary Report*, 3, <http://www.ands.gov.af/main.asp>.

17. UN Security Council Resolution 1659/2006, 15 Feb. 2006, <http://daccessdds.un.org/doc/UNDOC/GEN/N06/244/75/PDF/N0624475.pdf?OpenElement>.

18. Islamic Republic of Afghanistan, *The Afghanistan Compact*, 2, <http://www.ands.gov.af/main.asp>.

19. See documents at 5 and 6.

20. *Afghanistan's Endangered Compact*, 10–13.

21. Government of Canada, "Canadian Forces Operations in Afghanistan," *National Defence Backgrounder*, 25 Nov. 05, <http://www.forces.gc.ca/site/newsroom/view_news_e.asp?id=1703>.

22. Conversation between BGen David Fraser (CA), Comd RC (S), and author, 11 Feb. 2006.

23. Government of Canada, *National Defence Backgrounder*.

24. Ibid.

25. Joseph Collins, "Afghanistan: Winning a Three Block War," *Journal of Conflict Studies* (Winter 2004): 70–72.

26. Interview with David Mulroney by Robert Parkins and Chris Thatcher in *Vanguard*, July/Aug. 2007, <http://www.vanguardcanada.com/Common NarrativeMulroney>. [24 Aug. 2007].

27. Hammes, *The Sling and Stone*, 2.

28. "Don't Fail Afghanistan: Iraq May be Hopeless, but Afghanistan is Worth Defending. Here's Why and How," Editorial, *Los Angeles Times*, 27 Aug. 2007, <http://www.latimes.com/news/opinion/la-ed-afghanistan27aug27,0,3029831.story?coll=la-opinion-center> [27 Aug. 2007].

29. See Rohde and Sanger, "How a 'Good War' in Afghanistan Went Bad," for a wide-ranging description of the strategic confusion that permeates the American effort.

30. See John A. Nagle, *Counterinsurgency Lessons from Malaya and Vietnam: Learning to Eat Soup with a Knife* (Westport, CT: Praeger Publishers, 2002), for a description of the committee structure used by the British civil-military chain of command during the Malayan emergency.

No Room for Humanitarianism in 3D Policies: Have Forcible Humanitarian Interventions and Integrated Approaches Lost Their Way?

Stephen Cornish

ABSTRACT

This paper reviews the evolution of integrated and 3D approaches and highlights the different responses to such approaches shown by classic humanitarian organizations and multi-mandate development organizations. By providing an overview of past forcible humanitarian interventions and with a particular focus on Afghanistan, the practical and ethical challenges faced by aid agencies attempting to maintain programming in such contexts is traced.

In so doing, it will be suggested that the 3D approach emphasizing coherence between different instruments, while motivated by good intentions, has resulted in humanitarian and development aid programming becoming counterproductively subordinated to political interests. In fact, the co-optation of soft power for political and military ends in Afghanistan has led to reduced humanitarian assistance for populations in danger and to increased insecurity for humanitarians trying to assist them – thereby effectively exposing clear limits to the deeper integration strategies currently being promoted for stabilizing failed states.

INTRODUCTION

From an aid worker's perspective, the challenges and opportunities associated with civil-military coordination are seen in the context of the evolution from the tradition of neutral humanitarian assistance to the more controversial (yet now widely accepted) practice of forcible humanitarian interventions (HI). Arguably this ideological progression has removed the primacy of the *humanitarian imperative* and a victim's right to assistance according to need and supplanted it with a concept of aid as justice and as a tool for promoting peacebuilding and human security agendas.

With this shift, *soft power*[1] was brought into the tool kit to bring peace and security to failed and failing states, and "best theory" (versus "best practice") evolved, suggesting that greater scale, impact, and conflict transformation itself could be achieved through a more coherent

---

Particulars of Original Publication:
Reprinted with permission of the *Journal of Military and Strategic Studies* (Fall, 2007). Available online from <http://www.jmss.org/2007/2007fall/index.htm>.

or integrated use of security, political, development, and humanitarian assets. The use of integrated approaches for HIs was initially resisted at the United Nations (UN) by the United States (US) and some other allied states that were generally unwilling to play the role of the world's *humanitarian policemen*. However, the space and precedence set by the expanded legitimacy of *just forcible interventions* was closely watched within military circles that were rather more interested in co-opting soft power and assistance capabilities into their own defence strategies than in being co-opted into peacekeeping and peace-enforcement missions in what seemed to be, from a purely security-driven policy perspective, inconsequential failed and failing states.

Unexpectedly (and before these integrationist shifts in major donor countries represented by 3D policies [coordinated defence, diplomacy, and development efforts] could work out effective patterns of mutually beneficial communication, coordination, and co-operation), and just as the new normative frameworks were emerging onto the world's stage, the events of 9/11 occurred and the war on terror was launched. This resulted almost immediately in a number of defensive and pre-emptive war fighting missions that became heavily influenced over time by 3D approaches and which, for the most part, were quickly dressed in human rights and humanitarian clothing.

This paper reviews the evolution of these integrated approaches as they pertain to humanitarians and highlights the different responses to 3D policies by classic humanitarian organizations and multi-mandate development organizations. By providing an overview of past forcible interventions, but with a particular focus on the heightened difficulties present in Afghanistan, we trace the practical and ideological challenges faced by aid agencies attempting to maintain quality independent programming in such contexts.

In so doing, it is suggested that the current forms of integrated or 3D missions emphasizing coherence between different instruments, while motivated by good intentions, have resulted in humanitarian and development aid programming becoming subordinated to political interests in counterproductive ways. In fact, we will see how the co-optation (both willing and otherwise) of soft power has led to reduced humanitarian assistance in a number of conflict settings, including those in the war on terror, and to increased insecurity for both populations in danger and for the very humanitarians trying to assist them.

It is also argued that this state of affairs has led aid workers and NGOs to resist this bigger agenda, as they see it undermining the entire purpose and goals of humanitarianism and the motives that drive humanitarian and development work. Unfortunately, by questioning the politicization of aid and the notion of shared goals (commonly ascribed) amongst all 3D actors, humanitarians are now seen as obstructionist and antiquated by the political and military communities.

Multi-mandate organizations, as entities committed both to providing relief (according to independent humanitarian principles) and carrying out development programming which can be seen as supporting the political interests of host governments and/or of donor governments, are caught in this paradox. As such, they have had to adapt their principles and accept certain operational constraints in order to work in proximity to 3D missions. With presence, however, comes a duty to bear witness to the populations' suffering and to uphold international humanitarian law (IHL), something which may conflict with the short-term operational or strategic concerns of other members of the coordinated approach.

Ultimately, the article argues that there are limits to coherence and aims to give all 3D actors a better understanding of these limitations to deeper integration, especially in settings of open conflict and insecurity. It also hopes to promote a renewed sense of purpose to clarify and implement civil-military communication protocols that will protect both civilians and aid workers and truly respect and promote humanitarian space.

HOW WE GOT HERE: FROM HUMANITARIAN ASSISTANCE TO FORCIBLE HUMANITARIAN INTERVENTION

The 1990s would prove to be a period where humanitarianism was absorbed by politico-military responses to conflict, which some would argue often failed the very civilians the operations were ostensibly launched to protect. In this period, the inviolability of state sovereignty would be challenged and the concept of human security would emerge, eventually leading to forcible military intervention, not only to protect civilians in the short-term, but to set the stage for integrated, coordinated, and coherent approaches to conflict transformation and democracy building.

In 1991, several hundred thousand Kurds fled to Turkey and Iran in response to brutal suppression by Saddam Hussein. The Security Council declared the situation a "threat to international peace and security" under chapter VII of the *UN Charter.*[2] The resulting military intervention, deemed humanitarian by the UN and by the British, French, and American interveners,[3] saw the establishment of a safe haven that provided humanitarian assistance to the displaced and allowed those who took refuge in neighbouring states to return home.

This politico/military/aid intervention in Northern Iraq came on the heels of the UN's own International Humanitarian Commission's independent report of 1987, which stated that sovereignty should not be allowed to trump humanitarian considerations and that humanitarian corridors should be established by force if necessary to allow for the delivery of humanitarian assistance to the victims of armed conflict. What began as a defensive war to expel Iraqi forces from Kuwait was then turned into a so-called humanitarian intervention after the Kurdish forces, who were encouraged to rise up by their US benefactors, were abandoned by them militarily and then suffered harsh reprisals at the hands of the remnants of Saddam Hussein's forces.[4]

A number of NGOs who intervened to provide aid were thus either knowingly or unknowingly co-opted by the US forces in this effort to meet the Kurds' very real needs. Unfortunately, as the donor and/or party to the conflict was complicit in creating these needs, the assistance should have been offered as compensation or been deemed to be the obligation of the party to the conflict and should not have been portrayed as humanitarian in nature.[5]

Operation Provide Comfort was offered up as proof that political, military, and aid actors could function together in a coordinated manner not only to reduce suffering, but more encouragingly, to protect civilian populations in danger. With what appeared to be a successful precedent in hand, the way was now paved for the foundation of the integrated approach outlined in Boutros Boutros-Ghali's 1992 *Agenda for Peace* in which "the UNSG called for the mobilization of political, military, and aid assets in a coherent manner to build peace and security."[6]

This Iraqi success story, however, was then followed by two colossal HI failures in Bosnia and Somalia, which would tragically show the limitations of traditional UN peacekeeping's ability to provide civilian protection and would highlight the unwillingness of states or coalitions to put their soldiers in harm's way for the cause of protecting civilians and ensuring access to humanitarian assistance.

Furthermore, the reluctance to deploy sufficient troop strength and the low tolerance for assuming casualties in such operations led to defensive or tentative postures and to reliance on air power which can inflict a heavy toll on the very civilian population that the mission is intended to protect:

> There is a problem that seemed to stalk all interventions with a basically humanitarian purpose in the 1990s. The Western powers that were willing to intervene militarily were reluctant to accept the risk of casualties. This leads to particular modes of operation, such as hesitant and temporary military involvements and reliance on air power, which may conflict with the supposed humanitarian aims of the operation.[7]

David Rieff suggests that the above-mentioned HI failures crystallized a new, albeit unofficial, intervention policy in which "instead of political action backed by credible threat of military force, the Western powers would substitute a massive humanitarian effort to alleviate the worst consequences of a conflict they wanted to contain."[8]

It is in this context that the tragedy of the Rwandan Genocide would thus be allowed to occur, with the UN actually reducing troop numbers rather than strengthening the force (as Dallaire had recommended) prior to the height of the violence. This allowed the worst of the atrocities to unfold – witnessed by a woefully inadequate and ineffectual humanitarian community – sponsored by the donors' *cheque-book diplomacy.*

More moderate authors suggest that the inaction in Rwanda actually forced the international community to admit that although it wished to intervene to stop human suffering (on purely humanitarian grounds), it could garner the funds, troop strength, and political will needed only when the individual troop-contributing nations had additional national-interest-based justifications for deploying troops and participating in the humanitarian intervention or robust peacekeeping endeavour,[9] such as maintaining regional influence or preventing flows of refugees.

These early HIs and the Rwanda experience set in motion a process of re-examination at the UN which strengthened the idea of using force to guarantee civilian protection where it was seen wanting and to enforce peace and fight wars[10] when ethnic cleansing and genocide were suspected. In this way, the UN and the community of nations would live up to the cries of "never again" that followed the genocide.

By the end of the decade of the 1990s, HIs would make a comeback in which humanitarian actors would be confronted by the paradoxical means used by the international community to achieve these desired ends. In Kosovo, NGOs were confronted with the oxymoron of humanitarian war where aerial bombardments would initially increase the number of IDPs (internally displaced peoples) and add flame to the conflict. This does not imply that some wars are not just: humanitarians called for military intervention in Rwanda to stop the genocide because it was political, not humanitarian, action that was required.[11] In Sierra Leone, agencies were discouraged from assisting thousands of acutely malnourished people held hostage along the border in Kailahun until political advances allowing UN peacekeepers to return to the region could be made. In Liberia, ECOMOG helicopters fired on MSF relief aid convoys who were openly transgressing a UN-sanctioned food aid blockade that was imposed to weaken Taylor's regime.

While Kosovo, Sierra Leone, and Liberia ultimately have since been stabilized and a new age of hope has resulted, in all cases the long-term benefits of peace and protection were often reached by sacrificing the emergency protection and assistance needs of large segments of the population. This ethical dichotomy which promotes peace ahead of the humanitarian imperative would leave lasting scars that would ultimately divide the humanitarian community and shape its willingness to co-operate in future interventions.

Before addressing the progression from HIs to 3D policies, it is perhaps best to focus our discussion on the aid agencies and their experience in complex emergencies and in HIs.

The Trials and Tribulations Faced by Aid Agencies in War and the Promise of Conflict Transformation

Traditionally, international NGO (hereafter INGO) presence in war zones was undertaken to provide humanitarian assistance to long-suffering civilian populations. That populations have a right to assistance without discrimination is one of the fundamental principles of the humanitarian imperative and is enshrined in both International Humanitarian Law (IHL) and in the Geneva Conventions. In order to gain access to war zones and to create the humanitarian space necessary for delivering assistance safely and for providing some degree of protection for the beneficiaries, principles of neutrality, impartiality, and independence were devised:

> This is because the fundamental principle of independence, impartiality and neutrality not only characterizes humanitarian action's single-minded purpose of alleviating suffering unconditionally and without ulterior motive ... [these principles] also serve as operational tools that help in obtaining the consent of belligerents and the trust of communities for the presence and activities of humanitarian organizations, particularly in volatile contexts.[12]

These classical humanitarians (now known as minimalists) were joined by increasing numbers of development NGOs in the complex emergencies and conflict zones in the post-Cold War period. As such, together they faced the challenges of obtaining mission security in intra-state conflicts and of negotiating humanitarian space with non-state actors, and they watched the horrors that resulted from ineffectual peacekeeping missions and the early HIs that were deployed. They also lived the high mortality rates in the Rwandan refugee camps that they were unable to prevent, and they watched as aid was appropriated by armed groups intent on using it for political gain.

As a result of these inadvertent negative impacts of humanitarian assistance, leading aid organizations came together to define codes of conduct in aid, best practices, and minimum standards for assistance. The 1995 *Red Cross Code of Conduct* that emerged was established to uphold humanitarian behaviour and independence and to prevent abuses and the appropriation of humanitarian assistance (including the overt politicization of aid), which is spelled out in one of its principal tenets:

> We will never knowingly – or through negligence – allow ourselves, or our employees, to be used to gather information of a political, military, or economically sensitive nature for governments or other bodies that may serve purposes other than those which are strictly humanitarian, nor will we act as instruments of foreign policy of donor governments.[13]

Under the code, agencies would still be able to implement programs in conjunction with governments, if the aid agencies' goals were res-pected (or co-aligned naturally, as is often the case in responding to natural disasters), when the principle of allocating aid according to need was upheld, and when humanitarian motivations for assistance could be guaranteed. In addition to the code governing intentions, a convention dealing with aid effectiveness would set out minimum technical standards for aid delivery in order to ensure quality aid for the populations being assisted. The largest and most influential of these forums became known as the Sphere Project.[14]

Interestingly, humanitarian best practices for aid delivery were established through medical evaluation, epidemiological studies, and years of field practice that were then compiled and used to set the standards for aid organizations responding in emergencies (unlike some more recent additions to best practices in integrated approaches, which are more akin to best theories). A recent study published in the *Lancet* medical journal attests to the fact that the last decade witnessed a significant decrease in morbidity and mortality in refugee camp settings and attributes this to adherence to the emergency guidelines and standards promoted by the Sphere Project.[15]

This introspective trend included the do-no-harm approach popularized by Mary B. Anderson, who argued that aid should not only be delivered responsibly, minimizing its impact on the conflict, but that it should also "help war to end by lessening intergroup tensions and strengthening intergroup connections."[16] Many INGOs operating in war zones have taken these ideas on board and are now "conflict proofing" their operations and seeking to empower local individuals and organizations.

Alongside the above-mentioned movement came the broadening of the conception of security from the classical state-centric view to one that included the notion of human security where a population's right to safety and basic needs would be safeguarded, also known as the human needs approach.

> The broadening of the concept of security also paved the way for the idea of aid as "peacemaker". Analysis of the causes of conflict shifted from a focus on competing ideologies, to a focus

> on poverty, environmental decline, and population growth; all areas in which aid actors could claim a particular competence.[17]

One of the main tenets underlying the coherent approach is the belief that only by tackling the root causes of conflict could wars be ended and peace restored. Integrated responses call for ending conflicts, maintaining peace, carrying out security, enacting economic reforms, and so on; [18] in these responses, the humanitarian imperative may be subsumed to the greater gains of long-term peace.

A number of development and multi-mandate organizations that were increasingly present in the complex emergencies of the 1990s had become disillusioned with what has been termed mere humanitarianism. Frustrated with temporary or band-aid solutions to long-term suffering and incensed by ineffectual peacekeeping missions that could offer precious little protection to the civilian populations or to the development agencies trying to assist them, these agencies took comfort in the integrationist promises of not only effectively reducing suffering in the short-term but of transforming these conflicts through long-term development and governance assistance.

Integrationist-leaning aid agencies believed that humanitarian space and the security of civilians could most effectively be achieved by outside military interventions. This model garnered the most vocal support from British and American aid organizations, some of which had argued for strong military involvement to accompany conflict resolution, reconstruction, and development.[19] These military, political, and assistance missions were seen as potential conflict transformers; these builders of a new peaceful order and their intervention model have become known as advocates of the maximalist approach.

This being said, it is important to stress that when humanitarian NGOs called for forcible intervention to restore calm, protect civilians, and assist aid delivery, "they are evoking a so-called police action of robust UN peacekeeping missions, not war." [20]

This maximalist approach emerged as human rights-based agendas were gaining prominence with liberal-minded governments in power in Washington, London, and Ottawa and when stronger co-operation with government on policy fronts led to successes such as numerous campaigns to ban landmines, the adoption of the International Criminal Court, and other similar initiatives. The governments in power were serious about the desire to consult with civil society organizations (CSOs) and wanted to tap into their credibility, their knowledge, and their constituencies. For NGOs, accepting a seat at the table could lead to more influence and better access to funding, but most importantly, it held out the promise of long-term impact through co-operation in integrated peacebuilding efforts.[21]

NGOs WORKING "IN" CONFLICT AND WORKING "ON" CONFLICT

The approach of the minimalists or the mitigation group of INGOs that concentrate their attention on securing humanitarian access, delivering quality assistance impartially, and reducing the unintended consequences of their aid – basically a mixture of classic humanitarianism influenced by the do-no-harm form of humanitarianism described above – has come to be known as "working *in* conflict."[22] These agencies rely on the primacy of the humanitarian imperative to guide their actions; conflict resolution or peacebuilding potential or benefits are positive side effects of their interventions and are not necessarily seen as goals in and of themselves.

In contrast, INGOs influenced by the maximalist or preventative ethic (which sometimes carry out the same types of programmes as do the minimalists) are actively seeking to reduce violence and encourage peaceful mechanisms for dispute resolution. This new approach, which has become known as "working *on* the conflict," calls for refocusing assistance projects to deal with the root causes of conflict, that is, supporting mediation efforts and strengthening protection for civilians and respect for human rights.[23]

This model rejects the old split between relief aid and development aid and suggests that properly placed development assistance can continue during the various phases of a conflict and can actually help to encourage the forces of peace.

Through the trials and tribulations of the 1990s, both the minimalist and maximalist NGOs had become convinced of the need for better coordination of assistance in conflict areas and of the need to reduce the unintended negative consequences of aid. While classic humanitarians sought to perfect their aid delivery and reaffirm their independence, some maximalists were undertaking peacebuilding programs and prepared to take a seat at the table in order to influence long-term conflict transformation.

THE EVOLUTION OF THE COHERENCE AGENDA: FROM UN INTEGRATED APPROACH TO 3D WAR

> Canadian interest in more integrated policy responses to fragile and post-conflict states reflects in large measure the perceived lessons of peace operations during the 1990s, particularly in the Balkans and Africa, which highlighted the limitations of uncoordinated approaches to security, governance, and development in war-torn societies.[24]

The whole-of-government approach (WGA)[25] (or 3D approach, as it was originally known in Canada) is intended to have sustainable impact and is focused on fostering peace, security, economic resurgence, and good governance. Working together as equal partners, the various arms of donor governments and others (like aid agencies) are intended to act not only to resolve conflict but also to transform societies, lifting failed and failing states into a new era of responsible governments that serve their people's best interests.

In their review of WGAs, Patrick and Brown found that such partnerships worked best amongst "partnerships of equals," and that the growing pains of different agencies coming together to build shared views and response strategies had been a slow and painful process on the ground. In fact while the actors may be attempting to co-operate and/or coordinate in a partnership model in good faith, there has yet to be agreement amongst them on both the definition and the utility of the key organizing concept of a *failed state*.[26]

In fact, in the absence of an agreed-upon definition, development agencies and liberal-minded governments were promoting a development agenda for failed states while conversely, departments of defence (including Canada's) and more conservative governments were concentrating on the security dimensions.

In the US Defense Department's view, coherent approaches are actually nothing short of a new national security strategy aimed at overcoming new challenges and threats and winning the irregular and unconventional wars of the post-Cold War era. Having assessed its traditional military capacity as being ill-suited to face the new conflicts alone, it has called for a new "unified statecraft" which is "much more than mere coordination"; it requires a "seamless integration of federal, state, and local capabilities at home and among allies, partners, and non-governmental organizations abroad."[27] Only by developing this new statecraft along with generating additional concepts of interagency and international co-operation will the US effectively meet the challenges of the twenty-first century, it is argued.

Although perhaps shocking upon first review, the combined benefits of stability, democracy, and economic opportunities that could theoretically be created by such an approach could nonetheless still be seen as justified in exceptional cases by some maximalists, assuming all partners have a voice and some influence over the strategies and policies to be adapted and put into place. The massive asymmetries in both policy influence and resources that the US Department of Defense has over the US Agency for International Development (USAID), for example, ensures that no level playing field can exist, and that the interests and priorities of the latter will almost always be subsumed to the primary player.[28] We will return to this theme later when dealing with the co-optation of the third D (that of development) under the war on terror, where defence actors seek to control, rather than to consult, the other actors involved in the WGA agenda.

For the non-aligned movement, the US Department of Defense's viewpoint only served to confirm its long-held suspicions that Western human right priorities and HIs were nothing more than fronts for eroding state sovereignty and for promoting largely northern defence priorities. With southern states voicing opposition[29] and with the controversial use of force in the HIs in both Bosnia and Kosovo still proving divisive, the future of UN-led HIs appeared to be in difficulty.

Sensing this state of affairs, Kofi Anan put out a call to "forge unity" around the issue of HIs. The result was the International Commission on Intervention and State Sovereignty's (ICSS) September 2000 report, *The Responsibility to Protect* (R2P), which sought to establish guidelines for military interventions and promoted the concept and indeed the responsibility of member states to intervene to protect populations in danger from their own governments.[30]

Canada realized early on that forcible interventions could be used to do harm as well as good, and that the rules and practices governing its implementation would be key in setting the normative policy framework for its usage.[31] It sought to position itself at the forefront of efforts to formalize the rules governing future HIs, an effort which eventually would lead to the UN's adoption of the R2P doctrine.[32]

Unfortunately, the culmination of these efforts by Canada and other like-minded governments came inauspiciously in the aftermath of 9/11. As a result, the R2P draft approved would see the inclusion of threat-based interventions and would entrench the Security Council as the ultimate arbiter of interventions (rather than the General Assembly, as was initially intended). Arguably, the very intent to prevent and protect populations from suffering at the hands of their own governments and the effort to instill a duty on the part of nations to intervene in failed states on humanitarian grounds was seen to have been subsumed to the "West's concerns for its own population's safety and national security."[33]

It was at this juncture that the treatment of failed states openly became driven by national security agendas and where the fissure separating the varied definitions of failed states was erased, with poverty reduction, development, and the rights-based approach officially being subordinated to wider strategic imperatives. While this may have been inevitable, it nonetheless exposed a lack of shared goals amongst the 3D actors and would further erode their ability to coordinate effectively in theatre.

While the US had long viewed WGAs on security grounds, as did many national defence and security agencies (including Canada's[34]), the emergence of a new global threat allowed the normative justification and precedents for humanitarian interventions to be appropriated by the security agenda and to be used as a vehicle for pre-emptive and defensive war. For the US administration and the military, humanitarians were to serve as force multipliers (as was famously stated by Secretary of State Colin Powell[35]) in these new conflicts, and their actions coordinated and controlled to ensure strategic benefit and force acceptance.

Even oversees development aid (ODA), which has been a staunch supporter of the rights of the poor, has been distorted by the "security lens" through which many Western governments now view the world and its failed and failing states.

> In the post 9/11 world security-centric era, poverty and violent conflict in the South are viewed increasingly as "threats" to the security of the North. Development assistance is once again seen through the lens of northern foreign policy interests, as a tool for rich countries to defend themselves against these "threats".[36]

It was precisely this type of national security and *threat lens* which prompted many nations to join the International Security Assistance Force (ISAF) which would come in support of the US-led war on terror in Afghanistan: their primary task was to seek to redress the failed state in order to prevent a relapse into the chaos which had reigned, seemingly unchallenged, under the Taliban.

Transforming Afghanistan: From the War on Terror to Peacebuilding

Following the initial success of the US-led invasion of Afghanistan, a two-year opportunity for reconstruction and development existed and was essentially wasted by the interveners:

> A window of opportunity existed between 2002–2004 even in the Pashtun tribal areas for the United Kingdom and the United States to have made marked impact on development and reconstruction. One billion (dollars) was delivered, much of it usurped by contractors and warlords. The population's frustration began to grow and boiled over with the winter of 2004 (the coldest in twenty years) in which thousands of Afghans, many of them children, perished while the West continued security payments to the warlords and attention turned to other adventures.[37]

Much like the earlier US-led operation in Northern Iraq, the invasion of Afghanistan has gone from being seen as a combat operation called Operation Enduring Freedom to being seen as a UN-sanctioned, NATO-led, whole-of-government, forcible, military intervention aimed at stabilizing a failed state, reconstructing a war-ravaged country, and providing the long suffering Afghan population with economic opportunity, good governance, and the rule of law.

For NGOs – and arguably for most peacebuilding practitioners – peacebuilding is seen as a transversal process with an emphasis on grassroots (or bottom-up [Track III]), inclusive, common-ground activities which complement Track I activities like peacekeeping, governmental negotiations, and planning, and on Track II mediation and facilitation work conducted by NGOs, religious leaders, and academics.[38]

An argument can even be made that while all levels of peacemaking and peacebuilding are important, most recent transitions towards peace have resulted from pressure that was "bubbling up from the grassroots."[39] In Afghanistan, however, we are witnessing an attempt at predominantly top-down societal transformation (imposed largely from the outside) coupled with the supporting role of the newly elected Afghan government.

The peace-enforcement and peacebuilding talked about is a bit of a misnomer as large parts of the country remain embroiled in full-scale conflict. Whether or not a negative peace (the absence of war) can be achieved militarily and positive peace (overcoming the issues which led to, or could lead to, renewed hostilities) secured through economic benefits of assistance remains to be seen. And while there is a belief amongst some practitioners that one can encourage conflicts to subside, the majority believe that a conflict must play itself out before a situation can be ripe for peacebuilding.

In the past, both peacekeepers and NGOs have come under scrutiny for reinforcing the *natural order* that created the conflict in the first place, leading to a severe questioning of UN-sanctioned peacebuilding and forcible interventions.[40] The latter are now more contentious, as they are seen as reinforcing the culture of violence – where the lesson retained is that the biggest guns win. As a result, for some NGOs, there is a question of confidence in the international efforts' ability to succeed in Afghanistan under these assumptions.

THE DILEMMAS FOR MULTI-MANDATE ORGANIZATIONS

Multi-mandate organizations, that is, those that work on both relief and development, are further affected as they attempt to promote peacebuilding and implement government-sponsored programming in more secure areas of the country. This dual role – not unlike the duality inside the UN agencies themselves – means such organizations are attempting to work *in* conflict by delivering humanitarian aid and to simultaneously work *on* the conflict itself through participating in, for example, the reintegration phase of the disarmament, demobilization, and reintegration (DDR) process.

Furthermore, with conflict resolution and peacebuilding activities, agencies are looking to work on the conflict itself and, as such, take on an additional set of risks, as Lederach points out:

> To be directly involved in peacebuilding activities in settings of violent conflict supposes a certain level of precariousness and risk (as in danger), and involves balancing very complex relationships. Peacebuilding represents sensitive, delicate, and at times, very confidential work where lives are on the line and affected by the actions taken.[41]

Even such seemingly benign and commonly practised activities as "conflict mapping" in order to better understand how aid may interact with the conflict may be misinterpreted by local actors, who may not understand why INGOs are looking into what appear to be strategic and military matters. The difficulties in responding to these challenges adequately are heightened under the integrated, or strategic, approach in Afghanistan where the line between politics, military intervention, and humanitarian assistance becomes deliberately blurred as assistance is used as a tool[42] to support the desired peace:

> The distinction between humanitarian, political, and military action becomes blurred when armed forces are perceived as being humanitarian actors, when civilians are embedded into military structures, and when the impression is created that humanitarian organizations and their personnel are merely tools within integrated approaches to conflict management.[43]

Multi-mandate organizations involved in peacebuilding in Afghanistan must thus take increased care to ensure they do not further blur the lines by creating the impression that they are one with the political military project underway.

The Challenges to Aid: Humanitarian and Development Actors in the War on Terror

Unfortunately the challenges for humanitarians (to say nothing of those faced by the general population) in Afghanistan have largely outweighed the benefits brought by the 3D approach to the conflict. The following are among the most important challenges:

1. Co-opting aid for security purposes.
2. Carrying out peacebuilding and development efforts in the war on terror.

3. Safeguarding humanitarian principles and ethics.
4. Civilian protection and use of force issues.

The Reality of Aid report, which comments on the state of global development by combining the views of some thirty countries, dedicated its 2006 issue to examining the impact of security and conflict on aid. Its authors concluded that donor-led, WGA approaches to interventions have "largely subsumed diplomacy and development interests and favoured defence or military responses" for managing conflict and for meeting the strategic goals defined by the donor governments involved.[44] This, they point out, is not only true in Haiti, Sudan, and Iraq, but in Afghanistan, as well! This is something that aid agencies on the ground know all too well.

Co-opting Aid for Security Purposes

> *"The incentives to dress hard military objectives in soft humanitarian clothing have been present from the start, regardless of the party in charge."*[45]

From the outset in Afghanistan, the US-led effort paid little heed to the laws of war, be it to the Geneva Conventions or to IHL[46]; it is thus not surprising that there should be a lack of respect for the existing civil-military co-operation guidelines or experience worked out in earlier UN forcible military interventions and integrated missions. Aid, it seems, was to be conceived as nothing more than a weapon in the war against terror.

Non-uniformed special services officers – intentionally or not – camouflaged themselves by adopting the white land-cruisers associated with aid agencies and by addressing local leaders and elders with promises of aid and assistance. These officers were also the eyes and ears of the military and utilized the access gained to collect information. In some areas, pamphlets promising aid in exchange for providing information on the Taliban were also dropped. "The confusion over the role of humanitarian workers that resulted from these and similar incidents severely jeopardized their security."[47]

The resulting confusion caused by this blurring of the lines between humanitarian and military action was seen as a primary factor in the assassination of five MSF aid workers in 2004. Following their deaths, a Taliban spokesperson stated that aid organizations were working for American interests and had thus become legitimate targets, which led MSF to quit Afghanistan after twenty-four years of presence.[48]

The above-mentioned semi-clandestine operations have now largely been replaced with a more formalized form of co-opting aid for essentially political and military purposes called provincial reconstruction teams (PRTs). These US-designed units (now adopted by the militaries comprising

ISAF) were originally tasked with coordinating humanitarian aid and aid actors, and often operated outside of pre-existing UN coordination mechanisms, and while their initial job descriptions did not mention carrying out aid projects themselves, they soon began functioning as "military-relief hybrids".[49]

> The CF (Coalition Force) is both a fighting force actively engaged in an anti-insurgency shooting war and a "hearts and minds" operation that provides relief and services to the local population in a manner that is functional to its military objectives.[50]

After their launch by the US in 2002, both the British and American forces openly considered their PRTs' so-called humanitarian aid as an instrument in the war against terror.[51] In their classic form, the PRTs reflect the theoretical construct of the Three Block War (3BW) that US General Charles Krulack posited in the late 1990s, in which the military would effectively be conducting combat operations on one block, separating belligerents (or peacekeeping) on another, and distributing humanitarian aid on a third – all in the same theatre and all within a few hours.[52]

Both the American and Canadian forces adopted this untested construct believing that the "third block" of visibly placed development would buy consent and force security. Unfortunately, they failed to realize that proper development requires both a skill set and know-how that their members might not necessarily possess as well as broad-based community consent from the outset. Learning these lessons the hard way has resulted in situations like the rebuilding of the Parwan school three times, first by the US following the invasion – and then twice by the Canadian PRT, once after it was burned by the Taliban and a second time after Canadian Forces destroyed it during renewed fighting.[53] While rebuilding a school it had bombed might appear as a good-will gesture by some, the wisdom of doing so in the wake of Human Rights Watch's report recommending that schools not be built after two hundred had been subject to attacks (including threats, beatings, executions, and buildings being burned) from those opposed to the politico-military project underway[54] must surely be questioned. Militaries engaging in hearts-and-minds type projects are in essence struggling for control of the civilian population, something which can end up making them targets in the on-going hostilities and should therefore be avoided.[55]

It must also be said that other states, like the Dutch and the Norwegians, have attempted to separate military roles from humanitarian tasks and to have their PRTs prioritize building, not buying, consent for their mission by strengthening relations with local officials and promoting pro-peace initiatives. The British forces, while maintaining the right to carry out quasi-development projects under their civilian-military coordination (CIMIC) activities, have civilianized their PRTs in order to guarantee better quality programming and to ensure that their activities are coordinated and do not occur in areas already served by aid agencies.[56]

While some measured improvements have come about and improved dialogue between NGOs and military actors in Kabul is now taking place, many militaries have refused efforts to be bound by constraints on their PRTs' quasi-development efforts. Thus, despite efforts to limit the blurring of the lines between military and humanitarian assistance by some militaries involved in NATO's peacebuilding mission, other member states and the ongoing OEF continue to transgress the line for tactical and strategic benefits.

In an effort to maintain their independence and in order to protect themselves from the perception of assisting the military projects in Southern Afghanistan, some agencies refused to consider funds to extend project activities in the area until the Canadian military agrees to conduct only security and policing activities there.[57] Meanwhile, in addition to the recent spate of largely politically motivated killings and kidnappings of aid workers in Afghanistan, a new trend has been reported to us by the Afghanistan NGO Security Office (ANSO), one in which aid workers are being stopped at unofficial insurgent checkpoints and searched (including computers and mobile phones) for any signs of co-operation with the government or coalition militaries.

The damage done is perhaps already irreparable; the perceptions that aid actors are merely emissaries of their countries' intervening military forces will not soon fade. Tragically, dozens more humanitarians have been killed, and the consent-based, impartial NGO assistance model worked out over decades has been erased, further reducing assistance and development prospects for the population.[58] One commentator suggests that

> Any political-military intervention that has a humanitarian component instantly stigmatises humanitarians and puts them in danger. The stigma remains long after the military has departed, affecting trust and confidence with which humanitarians are perceived, literally adding years to the process of reconstruction, reconciliation, and prosperity.[59]

Despite such grim prospects, the increased risk to aid workers, and the reduction in areas where they can safely and effectively work, a number of NGOs have stayed on and attempted to carry out their assistance missions under the less than favourable conditions afforded by the 3D approach in Afghanistan.

Carrying Out Peacebuilding and Development Efforts In the War on Terror

> Humanitarians would never deny that the creation of a stable peace is in everyone's best interest. However, they would also assert the need for humanitarian action to exist alongside peacebuilding efforts in order to uphold the principle of humanity and the protection of civilian life as the conflict rages.[60]

Inside Afghanistan there are largely two realities. The first exists in the central, north, and western regions where humanitarian agencies and multi-mandate organizations are, despite the relative insecurity, still able to carry out humanitarian assistance, development initiatives, and peacebuilding ventures.

In these areas, the world's focused attention on Afghanistan has, despite the challenges, resulted in a number of successes that are often overshadowed by the obstacles that remain. Government-led, donor-sponsored, and often, NGO-implemented programmes have resulted in more than 350,000 families accessing micro-finance and micro-credit initiatives, and 12,000 of Afghanistan's 24,000 municipalities benefiting from the establishment of community development counsels and the implementation of locally managed development initiatives made possible by the Afghan Government's National Solidarity Program.

The second reality concerns eastern, southern, and other areas of the country where aid agencies have largely had to withdraw or reduce their programming to insufficient remote-controlled efforts due to security constraints related to the ongoing war on terror:

> Reconstruction has been very slow in the South. The food aid system has failed, causing a severe famine. Much of the population of southern Afghanistan is alienated from ISAF. Unless these circumstance change, the Canadian mission in Kandahar will become less and less acceptable to the local population. Time is not on NATO and Canada's side.[61]

Perhaps as a result of such portrayals, the general consensus emerging is that the 3Ds are not working in Afghanistan, and furthermore, that its failings can largely be attributed to the ineffectual and unco-operative development D.

Ultimately NGOs receive and implement between 10 and 15 per cent of donor aid arriving in the country, yet they are increasingly being held responsible for all the development failures in the Afghan context. A blame game has arisen in which each actor points to the other as being responsible for the apparent failures of the WGA in Afghanistan.

Development projects funded through external support and often directed through private contractors and/or PRTs have been singled out as being particularly costly, wasteful, lacking in quality, and often not taking into account community needs.[62] As well, government-led efforts have been stalled by a nascent and corrupt bureaucracy that has been overloaded by donor funding, despite its inability to manage and support such a heavy programming burden.[63]

ISAF and NATO have felt let down by all the above as they decry the lack of visible development benefits, which they believe would shore up the population's support following their hard-won victories on the battlefields.

According to Jack Granatstein, "the enemy has been strong enough that the Government's and the Canadian Forces' commitment to the 3D approach has not been able to receive a fair trial," and the blame falls upon the fact that the open war fighting has constrained the PRTs to spending more time protecting themselves than assisting the Afghan people, to CIDA for being ineffectual, and to Canadian NGOs for refusing to co-operate with the military.[64] For Granatstein, the pushing of the other non-consequential Ds to the background during times of strategic necessity – or when the battles rage – is simply a logical state of affairs and to be expected. For him, like many integrationists, the benefits of peace-enforcement will arrive once the battles have been won.

For many NGOs and peacebuilders alike, it is precisely this type of *security first* logic that is at the heart of the problem and ultimately leads to what some term a *state-building paradox*.[65] This refers to the fact that short-term gains on the counter insurgency, counter narcotics, and war on terror fronts continually undermine community-based peacebuilding efforts and development initiatives that are ultimately required for a more peaceable future and for the Coalitions' eventual success. This paradox is especially acute when coalition operations have led to large-scale loss of civilian life and property, have fostered anti-government and anti-NATO sentiment, and have ultimately either ignored and/or been complicit in the reduction of humanitarian space.

Safeguarding Humanitarian Principles of Independence, Neutrality, and Impartiality

Reconciling military, diplomatic, and humanitarian objectives may be a more effective way of stabilizing failed and fragile states, but it also creates inevitable trade-offs and requires a high degree of collaboration.[66]

The questions are, What trade-offs should be made? and How much can one agree to suspend one's own morality and principles in order to arrive at the greater good? What has also been shown through the Afghan experiment is that the degree of collaboration needed sometimes remains higher than agencies can afford without becoming complicit in the militaries' agenda. The same difficulties can sometimes also arise when collaborating with governments in development and peacebuilding efforts.

To remain independent, agencies must remain in charge of where, and with whom, they work. Yet in government- or military-led peacebuilding efforts, agencies sometimes have little control over the types of projects and/or the locations where they will be implemented.

What is often not understood is that many multi-mandate agencies have already sacrificed a portion of their neutrality, impartiality, and independence by acting as implementing agencies for various Afghan ministries. Agencies have done this to ensure their ability to assist and to participate in the peacebuilding activities funded by the donors under the WGA logic.

In fact, more than 80 per cent of NGO activities in the country are already tied to government programmes. While good donorship principles oblige that a majority of funds be directed through multilateral organizations or into direct budgetary support to the host government, this shift has further disenfranchised many beneficiaries and shut down "key services not covered under the remit of the current government programmes."[67]

In the South, the few NGOs still able to function have clearly been unable to meet the lifesaving needs of the civilian population. Defence actors have both offered to extend protection to aid agencies[68] and have tried setting up Priority Development Zones (PDZs) in which security would be maintained by the coalition members. From the humanitarian side, there is little belief in the solutions offered, something that perplexes the military and further fixes the stereotype that humanitarians are somehow antiquated and that they selectively use neutrality as an excuse to avoid working with the military. Yet in southern Afghanistan, CARE's local partners have been approached and told that their aid is good for the local community and may continue, but that if they or the programmes they implement become associated with NATO forces, then they will make themselves a target. This is not an idle threat. During my recent visit, four Afghan de-miners protected by ISAF and four armed UN security guards protecting a reconstruction engineer were killed the same week.

CARE is responsible for the lives of some 800 national staff and their families and is helping hundreds of thousands of Afghans in twelve provinces. We do this successfully under the traditional model of arranging safety through community acceptance and local integration. In this scenario, one must weigh very carefully the expansion of ones' activities into areas where the conditions for safe and successful delivery of assistance programming no longer exist.

The reality is that aid agencies would make themselves targets by working in PDZs as they would be seen to have taken sides, thus evaporating the consent-based security and community acceptance model on which they rely to carry out their programming. It is thus no wonder that, "aid agencies are very nervous about working side by side with the military. When that happens, their impartiality in the eyes of the community has been lost,"[69] and with it, their ability to safely and effectively carry out bottom-up, inclusive programming for the benefit of all.

Compromising on impartiality leads to the conditionality of assistance and the discrimination towards victims that has become a hallmark of the way the WGA and the Afghan government distributes and relates to development issues and assistance.

> As with many aid efforts, however, help for the displaced has been hampered by the Afghan government itself. Last March, the government declared that support for the camp dwellers should stop, so the people would be encouraged to return home. The WFP now plans to use its CIDA money to help get people out of the camps and back into their homes, with food-for-work incentives.[70]

Using food aid as a weapon to force civilians back into un-safe areas is clearly not something that any aid agency should support, yet contravening the ban risks bringing the ire of the Afghan authorities. That the WFP would be complicit in this points to the abrogation of its humanitarian mandate in favour of short-term political priorities.

In dealings the author had with one Afghan ministry (which will remain anonymous) when looking to begin programming in the volatile southern region, he was informed that the ministry intended to guarantee the organization's safety through the use of armed emissaries provided by the communities themselves. In cases where it was understood that security could not be guaranteed as a result of Taliban presence, the information would be transmitted back to ISAF and the Afghan National Army so that they could clean up the area, after which, assumedly, we would be encouraged to commence our programming. Extending the writ of the government's programming and assisting to rout out the Taliban thus went hand-in-hand in the eyes of the high-level ministry official in question.

These kinds of practices – co-operating in such a government program, using food aid as a weapon, or carrying out programmes together with the PRTs – would put us in direct contravention of the *Red Cross Code of Conduct* that humanitarians and development agencies signed back in 1995 precisely to guard against the politicization and instrumentalization of aid. That our organization could not follow through with such an unethical bargain was never in question. It did, however, show the limits of deep integration and reconfirmed the wisdom of reaffirming the core humanitarian principle of independence of action.

Civilian Protection/Use of Force Issues (Just War and HIs)

> In the long history of legal debates about humanitarian intervention there has been a consistent failure to address directly the question of the methods used in such interventions. It is almost as if the labeling of an intervention as humanitarian provides sufficient justification in itself, and there is no need to think further about the aims of the operation or the means employed.[71]

UN-mandated and/or sanctioned forces, such as NATO's ISAF, become party to the conflict by engaging in forcible humanitarian interventions and peacemaking efforts, and as such, they must respect the rules of IHL. Therefore just means, proportionality of response to threats presented, and avoiding civilian targets and institutions when possible must accompany the other IHL duties of promoting independent humanitarian assistance, otherwise the UN and its allies will be in contravention of IHL and will thus forfeit the legitimacy of these HIs themselves.[72]

Following a spate of well publicized incidents in which US and coalition bombardments led to high numbers of civilian casualties, the UN released a report stating that so far in 2007 more civilians deaths were caused by allied and Afghan forces than by the insurgents.[73] The vast majority of recent civilian deaths in Afghanistan, however, are not related to individual soldiers' reactions on the ground in the fog of war. Civilian deaths are largely due to the coalition's increasing reliance on aerial bombardments[74] and long-range artillery support (as was done in Kosovo) to compensate for limited troop numbers[75] and in order to minimize coalition casualties:

> Scores of civilian deaths over the past months from the heavy US and allied reliance on air strikes to battle Taliban insurgents are threatening popular support for the Afghan government and creating severe strains within the NATO alliance.[76]

In addition to the loss of life, increased coalition activity in the South has led to an increase in IDPs and has caused wide-scale damage to civilian houses, wells, and other infrastructure, thus further aggravating the humanitarian situation on the ground. One such attack near Herat this past summer led to dozens of deaths (including civilians), created over 2,000 IDPs, and left 170 houses wholly or partially destroyed.

The US and NATO have now both acknowledged the problem – although arguably they see the problem more in terms of losing hearts and minds and potential ramifications for their own force security than one of following IHL and of guaranteeing civilian protection. There is also a steady stream of apologies issued from NATO and the US forces, which are generally followed by the justification that the insurgents are taking sanctuary or hiding amongst civilians. Such behaviour on the part of the insurgency is clearly a breach of IHL as are many other tactics it uses (such as suicide bombings, which must be condemned unreservedly). However, even in such cases as shielding, proportionality must be taken into account in the response. While this indeed is a high standard, to maintain its legitimacy it must nonetheless be upheld by the HI.[77]

There is some cause for hope here in the so-called "European exception": Holland, France, and other continental nations view their presence in Afghanistan more in terms of keeping the peace and nation building and thus are said to be uncomfortable with the force posture and collateral damage being caused.

The sanctity of human life and the right to assistance and protection are fundamental constructs of the humanitarian endeavour. When humanitarians are present when these constructs are transgressed, they have a duty to give voice to the victims and to bear witness to the suffering observed. "Where there is contact with the victims of catastrophe that is instigated or made worse by the direct or structural oppression by some humans or others, the ethical mandate of bearing witness in favour of the victims arises spontaneously."[78]

The Afghanistan Coordination Body for Afghan Relief (ACBAR), which includes both Afghan and international NGOs, has now felt it necessary to explicitly underline breaches in IHL it deems to have resulted from the means and use of force employed by the coalition and the OEF, while resolutely condemning the indiscriminate methods used by the insurgency:

> We strongly condemn operations and force protection measures carried out by international military forces in which disproportionate or indiscriminate use of force has resulted in civilian casualties. Such operations have frequently been carried out by forces or agencies outside NATO command, often American forces in Operation Enduring Freedom, and sometimes in conjunction with Afghan forces.[79]

Ultimately, agencies that remain despite the challenges have a duty to advocate or witness on the victims' behalf. They do so in hopes that the military and political leaders will put in place policies and practices which will allow the soldiers on the ground to conduct their activities in ways that will better protect the civilian population, something which ultimately should enhance rather than detract from the mission's general objectives of restoring peace and security and ultimately, stabilizing the failed state.

CONCLUSION

The co-optation of aid for political and military purposes in Afghanistan has resulted in an ever-expanding area of the country suffering from a politically aggravated, acute humanitarian emergency that largely goes unreported and unattended. Both humanitarian minimalists and multi-mandate maximalists (including Afghan NGOs and INGOs) have largely had to abandon the heaviest conflict areas, as their consent-based presence was eroded and their safety undermined by the coalition forces that posited aid conditionally, used aid as a tool, and unwisely took on the appearance of aid workers.

The numerous challenges faced by aid agencies under the 3D approach have been greater than in previous HIs and have, at times, seriously strained relations amongst the various actors. This has led many aid agencies to conclude that the moral overlap of goals to which they subscribed in order to participate in shared conflict transformation agendas is first, unworkable in heavily militarized 3D approaches, and secondly, untenable in war on terror settings.

Humanitarians and development agencies have thus had to distance themselves from the deeper coordination and command-and-control agendas of other actors in the integrated approach, and to reaffirm their adherence to humanitarian principles and the code of conduct in order to create ever shrinking pockets of humanitarian space where they can still function. In future, multi-mandate NGOs and others who have taken on the working on conflict agenda must remain more vigilant of their independence and retain the lesson that such activity (unless conducted for both sides) can have consequences which can negatively affect both their own ability to carry out humanitarian relief activities, and the ability of traditional humanitarian agencies who never subscribed to these maximalist goals.

Whilst maintaining independence, all actors involved in the 3D in Afghanistan must continue to forge a strong culture of communication. Sharing the same terrain as they do, development, defence, and diplomatic actors will all be better served through improved understanding of respective mandates, positions, and operational cultures. While some may be disappointed that deeper coordination, coherence, or control by one lead actor are not possible or desirable, it was in fact entirely predictable from the moment the security agenda overtook the protection agenda as the lead motive for intervention.

Predictably, the 3D approach has been dominated by the defence D. Whether this is due to its advantage in size and funding or to its "can do" mentality can still be debated. What is less in doubt is that PRTs based on the 3BW concept (which pre-dates the war on terror) were deployed early on in the conflict and were seen as essential components in the heavily militarized solution to Afghanistan's problems. They did not originate spontaneously as a result of the failings of the other Ds, as is sometimes maintained.

While research suggests that equal partnership amongst actors in the coherent approach is the key to success, it is increasingly difficult to see how such a level playing field could ever be created in Afghanistan.

In setting out the failure of leading with a heavily militarized solution to dealing with failed states and transforming these states through forcible transformation, Axworthy writes that "If one wants recent proof of the problems with this approach, just look at what happened in Afghanistan, where the warlords reign supreme. The population is faced with constant threats to their security, development is stymied, and the export of heroin is setting new records."[80] The pessimistic view of progress to date was not, as seems likely, penned in the past months, but almost five years ago.

Regrettably, Canadian politicians continue to echo Colin Powell's view of NGOs as force multipliers by selling the war at home as a combined 3D/humanitarian mission.[81] Instead of promoting such dangerous and short-sighted rhetoric, our politicians should instruct the military commanders to devise policies and practices which promote civilian protection and which safeguard humanitarian space.

Use of force issues are actually intensifying the population's suffering and undermining the coalition's efforts in Afghanistan. As a result, special care must be taken to reduce displacement, destruction, and death caused by aerial bombardments in civilian areas. A serious review of rules governing use of force could ultimately reduce civilian casualties and would, at minimum, ensure the respect of the just means principle, which is essential for maintaining the legitimacy of the NATO- and UN-sanctioned mission.

Consent, it seems, cannot be easily purchased through visible PRT-led reconstruction projects, even if they are well intentioned, as they are often shortsighted and can lead to civilian targeting by the insurgency. Both these facts are increasingly being registered by the soldiers on the ground and by the command structures of progressive-minded militaries which are beginning to alter their military and donor policies.

While the civilianization of military PRTs is a step in the right direction, it would be preferable for the military to completely break with the militarization of aid. Even if properly conducted, bringing aid in one hand with a gun in the other will continue to politicize the assistance provided and lead to perceptions that will ultimately further reduce humanitarian space. This is where the limits to civil-military guidelines and co-operation lie, as militaries are unwilling to discuss or forgo their ability to conduct such quasi-development activities in conflict settings. As a result, and until such a time as the theoretical 3D construct can make room for an independent and operational humanitarian H, it may indeed be best to simply remove the development D[82] from the equation.

While Afghanistan is the central issue today, much more is at stake. The very legitimacy of humanitarian interventions could be lost if the international community is not careful to safeguard the core principle of humanity. Morality matters, and both right intentions and just means are essential to upholding the legitimacy of HIs. Hopefully Canada, as one of the lead architects behind the Responsibility to Protect doctrine, with its potential to avoid conflict, alleviate suffering, and protect civilians from the abuses of their own governments, will heed the warning signs before it is too late. What is abundantly clear is that since the war on terror, there has yet to be an effective and justified intervention that can be called humanitarian, and this should give all 3D actors (defence, diplomacy, and development) cause to pause and reflect.

Acronyms

3BW	= Three Block War
3D	= Defence, Diplomacy, and Development
ACBAR	= Agency Coordinating Body for Afghan Relief
ANSO	= Afghanistan NGO Security Office
CSO	= Civil Society Organization
DOD	= Department of Defence
HI	= Humanitarian Intervention
HLP	= High-Level Panel
ICRC	= International Committee of the Red Cross
IDPs	= Internally Displaced Peoples
INGO	= International Non-governmental Organization
ISAF	= International Security Assistance Force
MDGs	= Millennium Development Goals
MSF	= Médecins Sans Frontières
NGO	= Non-Governmental Organization
OEF	= Operation Enduring Freedom
PRTs	= Provincial Reconstruction Teams
R2P	= Responsibility to Protect
SSR	= Security Sector Reform
UN	= United Nations
US	= United States
UNAMA	= United Nations Assistance Mission to Afghanistan
WGA	= Whole-of-Government Approach

NOTES

1. Joseph S. Nye Jr., "Transformational Leadership and U.S. Grand Strategy," *Foreign Affairs* 85, no. 4 (July/Aug 2006): 139–48.
2. Edward Mortimer, "Under What Circumstances Should the UN Intervene Militarily in a 'Domestic' Crisis?," in *Peacemaking And Peacekeeping for the New Century,* ed. O. Otunnu and M. Doyle (Lanham, MD: Rowman and Littlefield, 1998), 114–15.
3. Adam Roberts, "Humanitarian War: Military Intervention and Human Rights," *Journal of International Affairs*, no. 69 (1993): 436–37.
4. Fiona Terry, *The Paradox of Humanitarian Action: Condemned to Repeat*? (Ithaca, NY: Cornell University Press, 2002), 241.
5. Ibid., 241.
6. Joanna Macrae and Nicholas Leader, "The Politics of Coherence: Humanitarianism and Foreign Policy in the Post-Cold War Era," *Humanitaire – enjeux, pratiques et debats* 1 (Nov. 2000): 65.
7. Adam Roberts, "Humanitarian Principles in International Politics in the 1990s," in *Reflections on Humanitarian Action – Principle, Ethics and Contradictions,* ed. Humanitarian Studies Unit, 23–54 (London: Transnational Institute/Pluto Press with the Humanitarian Studies Unit and the European Commission Humanitarian Office [ECHO], 2001).
8. David Rieff, *A Bed for the Night – Humanitarianism in Crisis* (Toronto: Simon and Schuster, 2002).
9. Victoria Wheeler and Adele Harmer, eds., *Resetting the Rules of Engagement – Trends and Issues in Military-Humanitarian Relations,* Humanitarian Policy Group Research Report, Overseas Development Institute, Report 21 (Mar. 2006), p. 22, <www.relief.web.int> [27 July 2007].
10. The analogy is entirely suited, given that peace enforcement (under chapter VII of the UN Charter) is actually another word for war fighting, although ostensibly carried out with the humanitarian intention of re-establishing the conditions for peace and for civilian protection. Philip Wilkinson, "Sharpening the Weapons of Peace," in *Peacekeeping and Conflict Resolution,* ed. T. Woodhouse and O. Ramsbotham (London: Frank Cass, 2000), 73–74.
11. Terry, *The Paradox of Humanitarian Action*, 242.
12. Nicholas de Torrente, "Humanitaranism Sacrificed: Integration's False Promise," *Journal of Ethics and International Affairs* 18, no. 2 (2004): 6.
13. NB. The code, although conceived for disasters, also covers conflict interventions that are further regulated under IHL. *The Code of Conduct for the International Red Cross and Red Crescent Movement and NGOs in Disaster Relief,* International Federation of Red Cross and Red Crescent Societies (IFRC), Annex VI to the resolutions of the 26th International Conference of the Red Cross and Red Crescent societies, 1–6, (Geneva: IFRC, 1995), <www.ifrc.org/Docs/idrl/I259EN.pdf> [24 Sept. 2007].
14. *The Sphere Project: Humanitarian Charter and Minimum Standards in Disaster Response* was launched in 1997 and represents three things: a handbook, a broad process of collaboration, and an expression of commitment to quality and accountability. <http://www.sphereproject.org/>, [24 Sept. 2007].

15. Peter Salama et al., "Lessons Learned from Complex Emergencies over the Past Decade," *Lancet,* No. 634 (2004): 1801–03.
16. Mary B. Anderson, *Do No Harm: How Aid Can Support Peace – Or War,* (London: Lynne Rienner, 1999), 67.
17. Macrae and Leader, "The Politics of Coherence," 67.
18. Joel Charny, "Upholding Humanitarian Principles in an Effective Integrated Response," *Journal of Ethics and Humanitarian Affairs* 18, no. 2 (2004): 13.
19. Michael Pugh, ed. "The Social-Civil Dimension," in *Regeneration of War-Torn Societies,* (London: Macmillan, 2000), 117.
20. Rieff, *A Bed for the Night*, 328.
21. Lloyd Axworthy, *Navigating a New World, Canada's Global Future* (Toronto: Knoff, 2003), 153.
22. Jonathan Goodhand with Philippa Atkinson, "Conflict and Aid: Enhancing the Peacebuilding Impact of International Engagement," *International Alert* (2001): 36, <http://www.reliefweb.int/training/IA-Conflict-01oct.pdf> [30 Sept. 2007].
23. Ibid., 37.
24. Stewart Patrick and Kaysie Brown, *Greater than the Sum of Its Parts: Assessing "Whole of Government" Approaches to Fragile States* (New York: International Peace Academy Press, 2007), 58.
25. While there are more constrictive uses of WGA referring exclusively to joined-up government departments, we will hereafter use the term interchangeably with 3D, or the coherent approach. We do so because government aid policy set according to WGA priorities influences the type and distribution of programming and defines the actors (including development agencies) who will carry them out. Additionally, some commentators and institutes now use WGA when referring to 3D efforts.
26. "Generally speaking, the concept is most popular among development ministries, which use it to describe a subset of poor countries where weak governance and state capacity are impediments to pro-poor growth. Foreign and Defence ministries tend to be more sceptical, finding the term a distraction from concrete challenges and crisis response and post conflict reconstruction." Patrick and Brown, *Greater than the Sum of Its Parts*, 128–29.
27. US Department of Defense, *Quadrennial Defense Review Report,* 6 Feb. 2006, 83–84, <www.defenselink.mil/gdr/report/Report20060203.pdf> [25 July 2007].
28. Patrick and Brown, *Greater than the Sum of Its Parts*, 130.
29. The non-aligned movement (which makes up 80 per cent of the world's population) explicitly rejected the right to humanitarian intervention as a principle at their world summit in 2000 and again in 2003. Noam Chomsky, *Hegemony or Survival,* (New York: Henry Holt, 2003), 24.
30. Wheeler and Harmer, "Resetting the Rules of Engagement," 22.
31. Axworthy, *Navigating A New World*, 199.
32. Erin Simpson and Brian Tomlinson, "Canada: Is Anyone Listening?" in *Reality of Aid: Focus on Conflict, Security and Development Cooperation*, 2006, 20, <www.realityofaid.org> [26 July 2007].

33. "War to Peace Transitions," A Conference Report of the 8th Peacebuilding and Human Security Consultations, Ottawa, Apr. 2005.

34. Canada's International Policy Statement, "A Role of Pride and Influence in the World – DEFENCE" Department of National Defence, <www.forces.gc.ca> [26 Aug. 2007].

35. Colin L. Powell, "Remarks to the National Foreign Policy Conference for Leaders of Nongovernmental Organizations," Washington, DC, 26 Oct. 2001, <http://www.yale.edu/> [25 Sept. 2007].

36. Simpson and Tomlinson, "Canada: Is Anyone Listening?" 5.

37. Vani Cappelli, "Alienated Frontier," *ORBIS* (Fall 2005): 723–24, <www.fpri.org/orbis> [26 July 2007].

38. Hugh Miall, Oliver Ramsbotham, and Tom Woodhouse, *Contemporary Conflict Resolution* (Cambridge: Polity Press, 2004), 20.

39. Ibid., 58–59.

40 . Ibid., 59.

41. John Paul Lederach, *Building Peace: Sustainable Reconciliation in Divided Societies* (Washington, DC: US Institute for Peace Press, 1997), 132.

42. Haneef Atmar, Sultan Barakat, and Arne Strand, eds., *From Rhetoric to Reality: The Role of Aid in Local Peacebuilding in Afghanistan* (New York: INTRAC, 1998), 36–38.

43. Raj Rana, "Contemporary Challenges in the Civil-Military Relationship: Complementarity or Incompatibility?" *International Review of the Red Cross* 86, no. 55 (2004): 586.

44. "Reality of Aid," 2006, 1, <www.reality of aid.org> [26 July 2007].

45. Taylor Owen and Patrick Travers, "3D Vision. Can Canada Reconcile Its Defence, Diplomacy and Development Objectives in Afghanistan?" *The Walrus* (July/Aug. 2007): 49.

46. Wheeler and Harmer, "*Resetting the Rules of Engagement,*" 21.

47. Owens and Travers, "3D Vision," 44–49.

48. Ibid., 46.

49. Isabelle Bercq, "La militarisation de l'action humanitaire en Afghanistan," Note D'analyse, 2 (Groupe de recherche et d'information sur la paix et la sécurité, 9 May 2005), <www.grip.org/bdg/g4572.htlm> [20 Aug. 2007].

50. Antonio Domini et al. "Mapping the Security Environment: Understanding the Perceptions of Local Communities, Peace Support Operations and Assistance Agencies," Report commissioned by the UK NGO–Military Contact Group (New York: Feinstein International Famine Center; Medford, MA: Tufts University, 2005), 12.

51. Bercq, "La militarisation de l'action humanitaire en Afghanistan," 1.

52. "The rubric of 3BW offers the military a logical framework for the variance of their work in a way which makes sense to a combat-centric. However, 3BW was never developed as an operational strategy, but was a framework to try and understand the complexity of contemporary armed conflicts

and other insurgencies." Sarah Jane Meharg, "Three Block Wars and Humanitarianism – Theory, Policy, and Practice," Final Report (Ottawa: Pearson Peacekeeping Centre, 2006), 7.

53. Story collected by the author (under Chatam House rules), Calgary, 20 Mar. 2007.

54. Human Rights Watch, "Lessons in Terror – Attacks on Education in Afghanistan," July 2006, <http://www.hrw.org/reports/2006/afghanistan 0706/index.htm> [Aug. 2007].

55. It is my understanding that the Canadian, British, and American militaries continue to have school construction targets to meet at this time.

56. Domini, "Mapping the Security Environment," 14.

57. Rick Westhead, "Relief Groups Reject Afghan Projects," *Toronto Star,* 19 Oct. 2006.

58. "There has been a sharp rise in attacks against aid workers (28 NGO workers killed from January to August 2006, compared with 31 aid workers killed during the whole of 2005) and conversely, a reduction in areas where agencies are prepared to work ... This has triggered a vicious circle: the insecurity is preventing reconstruction and this in turn is fuelling the population's distrust of both the international community and the government." Holly Ritchie, "Aid Effectiveness in Afghanistan at a Crossroads," ACBAR Briefing Paper (Nov. 2006): 5, <www.reliefweb.int/library/document/2006.acbar-afg-oinov.pdf> [26 July 2007].

59. Ted Itani, "Politicization of Aid," *On Track* 12, no. 1, (Spring 2007): 3, Conference of the Defence Associations Institute, <http://www.cda-cdai.ca/seminars/2005/English%202005%20Agenda.pdf>.

60. Erin A Weir, "Conflict or Compromise: UN Integrated Missions and the Humanitarian Imperative," *KAIPTC Monograph,* No. 4, (2006): 37, <www.trainingforpeace.org> [Sept. 2007].

61. Gordon Smith et al., "Canada in Afghanistan: Is It Working?" *Canadian Defence & Foreign Affairs Institute,* 2007, 14, <www.cdfai.org> [Aug. 2007].

62. Hamish Nixon, "Aiding the State? International Assistance and the Statebuilding Paradox," Briefing Paper Series (Kabul: Afghanistan Research and Evaluation Unit [AREU], 2007), 9.

63. Ritchie, "Aid Effectiveness in Afghanistan," 6.

64. J.L. Granatstein, *Whose War Is It? How Canada Can Survive in the Post 9/11 World* (Toronto: Harper Collins, 2007), 214–15.

65. Nixon, "Aiding the State," 1.

66. Owen and Travers, "3D Vision," 46.

67. Ritchie, "Aid Effectiveness in Afghanistan," 7.

68. "At the other extreme, a few agencies and donor representatives chose to embed themselves with the PRTs or to travel alongside CF convoys for their protection. This approach was chastised as dangerous by most assistance agencies." Domini, "Mapping the Security Environment," 15.

69. Rick Westhead, "Relief Groups."

70. Graeme Smith, "'We Have to Act Faster,' CIDA Says. Officials Concede Canadian Aid Flows Slowly in Afghanistan," *Globe and Mail*, 21 Jan. 2007.
71. Roberts, "Humanitarian War," 51.
72. Francoise Saulnier-Bouchet, "Action Humanitaire entre droit de la guerre et Maintien de la Paix," *Les cahiers de Mars*, No. 166 (3rd trimester 2000): 6–7, <www.msf.fr> [Feb. 2005].
73. A recent UN report said 593 Afghan civilians have been killed by violence linked to insurgents this year. But more of those deaths, 314, were caused by ISAF or Afghan security forces than by insurgents." Kim Barker, "Afghan Civilians Caught in Crossfire," *Chicago Tribune*, 8 July 2007.
74. "This year in Afghanistan, American aircraft have dropped 987 bombs and fired more than 146,000 cannon rounds and bullets in strafing runs, more than was expended in both categories from the beginning of the American-led invasion in 2001 through 2004, the Air Force said." David S. Cloud, "US Airstrikes Climb Sharply in Afghanistan," *New York Times*, 17 Nov. 2006.
75. *Economist*, "Western Forces in Afghanistan – Unfriendly Fire," Editorial, *Economist*, 51, 23 June 2007.
76. Carlotta Gall and David E. Sanger, "Afghan Civilian Deaths Damaging NATO," *International Herald Tribune*, 13 May 2007.
77. Michael, N. Smith, "War Technology, and International Humanitarian Law," *HPCR Occasional Paper Series*, Harvard University, Program on Humanitarian Policy and Conflict Research, (Summer 2005), 37.
78. Xabier Etxeberria, "The Ethical Framework of Humanitarian Action," in *Reflections on Humanitarian Action – Principle, Ethics and Contradictions*, ed. Humanitarian Studies Unit, (London: Transnational Institute/Pluto Press with the Humanitarian Studies Unit and the European Commission Humanitarian Office [ECHO], 2001), 93.
79. Agency Coordinating Body for Afghan Relief, "Protecting Afghan Civilians: Statement on the Conduct of Military Operations," 19 June 2007, <http://www.acbar.org> [24 Aug. 2007]
80. Axworthy, *Navigating a New World*, 194.
81. Maxime Bernier, "Why We're in Afghanistan," Op-ed, *National Post*, 24 Sept. 2007.
82. Itani, "Politicization of Aid," 3.

Bibliography

Agency Coordinating Body for Afghan Relief (ACBAR). *Protecting Afghan Civilians: Statement on the Conduct of Military Operations.* 19 June 2007. <http://www.acbar.org> [24 Aug. 2007].

Anderson, Mary B. *Do No Harm, How Aid Can Support Peace – Or War.* London: Lynne Rienner, 1999.

Atmar, Haneef, Barakat Sultan, and Arne Strand, eds. *From Rhetoric to Reality: The Role of Aid in Local Peacebuilding in Afghanistan.* New York: INTRAC, 1998.

Axworthy, Lloyd. *Navigating a New World: Canada's Global Future.* Toronto: Knoff Canada, 2003.

Barker, Kim. Afghan Civilians Caught in Crossfire. *Chicago Tribune,* 8 July 2007.

Bercq, Isabelle. La militarisation de l'action humanitaire en Afghanistan. *Groupe de recherche et d'information sur la paix et la sécurité.* 9 May 2005. <www.grip.org/bdg/g4572.htlm> [20 Aug. 2007].

Bernier, Maxime. Why We're in Afghanistan. Oped section, *National Post.* 24 Sept. 2007.

Bhatia, Michael, Kevin Lanigan, and Philip Wilkinson. *Minimal Investments, Minimal Results: The Failure of Security Policy in Afghanistan.* Kabul: Afghanistan Research and Evaluation Unit, 2004.

Cappelli, Vani. Alienated Frontier. *ORBIS* (Fall 2005): 715–29. <www.fpri.org/orbis> [26 July 2007].

Charny, Joel. Upholding Humanitarian Principles in an Effective Integrated Response. *Journal of Ethics and Humanitarian Affairs* 18, no. 2 (2004).

Chomsky, Noam. *Hegemony or Survival.* New York: Henry Holt and Company, 2003.

Cloud, David, S. US Airstrikes Climb Sharply in Afghanistan. *New York Times,* 17 Nov. 2006.

Department of National Defence. *DEFENCE: Role of Pride and Influence in the World.* Canada's International Policy Statement. <www.forces.gc.ca> [26 Aug. 2007].

de Torrente, Nicholas. Humanitarianism Sacrificed: Integration's False Promise. *Journal of Ethics and International Affairs* 18, no. 2 (2004).

Domini, Antonio et al. *Mapping the Security Environment: Understanding the Perceptions of Local Communities, Peace Support Operations and Assistance Agencies.* Report commissioned by the UK NGO – Military Contact Group. New York: Feinstein International Famine Center; Medford, MA: Tufts University, 2005.

Easterly, William. *The White Man's Burden – Why the West's Efforts to Aid the Rest Have Done So Much Ill and So Little Good.* Toronto: Penguin Books, 2007.

Economist. Western Forces in Afghanistan – Unfriendly Fire. Editorial. *Economist,* 23 June 2007.

Etxeberria, Xavier. The Ethical Framework of Humanitarian Action. *Reflections on Humanitarian Action – Principle, Ethics and Contradictions,* ed. Humanitarian Studies Unit. London: Transnational Institute/Pluto Press with the Humanitarian Studies Unit and the European Commission Humanitarian Office (ECHO), 2001.

Goodhand, Jonathan and Philippa Atkinson. Conflict and Aid: Enhancing the Peacebuilding Impact of International Engagement. *International Alert* (2001).

Gall, Carlotta and David E. Sanger. Afghan Civilian Deaths Damaging NATO. *International Herald Tribune,* 13 May 2007.

Granatstein, J.L. *Whose War Is It? How Canada Can Survive in the Post 9/11 World.* Toronto: Harper Collins, 2007.

ICRC. *Summary of the Geneva Conventions of August 1949 and Their Additional Protocols.* Geneva: ICRC, 1983.

IFRC. *The Code of Conduct for the International Red Cross and Red Crescent Movement and NGOs in Disaster Relief: 1-6.* Annex VI to the resolutions of the 26th International Conference of the Red Cross and Red Crescent Societies held in Geneva in 1995. <www.ifrc.org/Docs/idrl/I259EN.pdf> [24 Sept. 2007].

Itani, Ted. Politicisation of Aid. *On Track* 12, no. 1 (Spring 2007): 21–27. Conference of Defence Associations Institute. <http://www.cda-cdai.ca/pdf/ontrack12n1.pdf>.

Kurth, James. Humanitarian Intervention after Iraq: Legal Ideals vs Military Realities. *ORBIS* (Winter 2005): 87–101. Foreign Policy Research Institute. <www.fpri.org/orbis/5001/kurth.humanitarianinterventionafteriraq.pdf> [26 July 2007].

Lederach, Jean Paul. *Building Peace: Sustainable Reconciliation in Divided Societies.* Washington, DC: US Institute for Peace Press, 1997.

Macrae, Joanna and Nicholas Leader. The Politics of Coherence: Humanitarianism and Foreign Policy in the Post-Cold War Era. *Journal Humanitaire – enjeux,pratiques et debats* 1, no. 11 (2000).

Miall, Hugh, Oliver Ramsbotham, and Tom Woodhouse. *Contemporary Conflict Resolution.* Cambridge: Polity Press, 2004.

Mortimer, Edward. Under What Circumstances Should the UN Intervene Militarily in a "Domestic" Crisis? In *Peacemaking and Peacekeeping for the New Century,* ed. O. Otunnu and M. Doyle. Lanham, MD: Rowman and Littlefield, 1998.

Nixon, Hamish. Aiding the State? International Assistance and the Statebuilding Paradox in Afghanistan. Afghanistan Research and Evaluation Unit – *Briefing Paper Series.* Kabul: Afghanistan Research and Evaluation Unit, 2007.

Owen, Taylor and Patrick Travers. 3D Vision – Can Canada Reconcile its Defence, Diplomacy, and Development Objectives in Afghanistan? *The Walrus* (July/August 2007).

Padilla, Arnold and Brian Tomlinson. Shifting Trends: ODA, Global Security and the MDG's. *Reality of Aid – 2006.* <www.realityofaid.org> [26 July 2007].

Patrick, Stewart and Kaysie Brown. *Greater than the Sum of Its Parts – Assessing "Whole of Government" Approaches to Fragile States.* New York: International Peace Academy Press, 2007.

Powell, Colin, L. Remarks to the National Foreign Policy Conference for Leaders of Nongovernmental Organizations. Washington, DC. 26 Oct. 2001. <http://www.yale.edu/> [25 Sept. 2007].

Pugh, Michael. The Social-Civil Dimension. In *Regeneration of War-Torn Societies.* London: Macmillan Press, 2000.

Rana, Raj. Contemporary Challenges in the Civil-Military Relationship: Complementarity or Incompatibility? *International Review of the Red Cross,* No. 86 (Sept. 2004): 855.

Rieff, David. *A Bed for the Night – Humanitarianism in Crisis.* Toronto: Simon and Schuster, 2002.

Ritchie, Holly. Aid Effectiveness in Afghanistan at a Crossroads. ACBAR Briefing Paper. 2006. <www.reliefweb.int/library/document/2006.acbar-afg-oinov.pdf> [26 July 2007].

Roberts, Adam. Humanitarian Principles in International Politics in the 1990s. In *Reflections on Humanitarian Action – Principle, Ethics and Contradictions*, ed. Humanitarian Studies Unit, 23–54. London: Transnational Institute/Pluto Press with the Humanitarian Studies Unit and the European Commission Humanitarian Office (ECHO), 2001.

––––. Humanitarian War: Military Intervention and Human Rights. *Journal of International Affairs* 69, no. 3 (1993).

Ross, Steven. *Breaking Point: Measuring Progress in Afghanistan.* Center for Strategic and International Studies. <www.csis.org/media/csis/pubs/070223_breakingpoint.pdf> [20 July 2007].

Salama, Peter et al. Lessons Learned from Complex Emergencies over the Past Decade. *The Lancet*, No. 634 (2004).

Saulnier-Bouchet, Francoise. Action Humanitaire entre droit de la guerre et Maintien de la Paix. *Les cahiers de Mars,* No. 166 (2000). <www.msf.fr> [Feb. 2005].

Schmitt, Michael N. War Technology and International Humanitarian Law. *HPCR Occasional Paper Series.* Harvard University, Program on Humanitarian Policy and Conflict Research. Summer 2005.

Simpson, Erin and Brian Tomlinson. Canada: Is Anyone Listening? *Reality of Aid.* 2006. <www.realityofaid.org> [26 July 2007].

Slim, Hugo. With or Against? Humanitarian Agencies and Coalition Counter Insurgencies. *Refugee Survey Quarterly* 23, no. 4 (2004): 34–47.

Smith, Gordon et al. *CanadaS in Afghanistan: Is It Working?* Calgary: Canadian Defence & Foreign Affairs Institute, 2007. <http://www.cdfai.org/PDF/Canada%20in%20Afghanistan%20Is%20it%20Working.pdf> [Aug. 2007].

Smith, Graeme. "We Have to Act Faster, CIDA Says." Officials Concede Canadian Aid Flows Slowly in Afghanistan. *Globe and Mail*, 21 Jan. 2007.

Terry, Fiona. *The Paradox of Humanitarian Action – Condemned to Repeat?* Ithaca: Cornell University Press, 2002.

US Department of Defense. *Quadrennial Defense Review Report.* 6 Feb. 2006. <www.defenselink.mil/gdr/report/Report20060203.pdf> [25 July 2007].

War to Peace Transitions Conference. A Conference Report of the 8th Peacebuilding and Human Security Consultations held in Ottawa, Canada, Apr. 2005.

Weir, Erin, A. Conflict or Compromise: UN Integrated Missions and the Humanitarian Imperative. *KAIPTC Monograph 4.0.* <www.trainingforpeace.org> [Sept. 2007].

Westhead, Rick. Relief Groups Reject Afghan Projects. *Toronto Star,* 19 Oct. 2006.

Wheeler, Victoria and Adele Harmer, eds. Resetting the Rules of Engagement– Trends and Issues in Military-Humanitarian Relations. Report 21. Humanitarian Policy Group Research, Overseas Development Institute. <www.relief.web.int> [Mar. 2006].

Wilkinson, Philip. Sharpening the Weapons of Peace. In *Peacekeeping and Conflict Resolution*, ed. T. Woodhouse and O. Ramsbotham. London: Frank Cass, 2000.

Civil-Military Coordination Practices and Approaches within United Nations Peace Operations

Cedric de Coning

ABSTRACT

This paper argues that the bi-polar civil-military coordination concept is no longer adequate to describe the system-wide coordination needs of contemporary United Nations (UN) peace operations at the strategic level in the context of the UN integrated mission concept. However, the civil-military coordination concept is still appropriate and meaningful at the operational and tactical levels, both from a humanitarian and a military perspective. UN civil-military coordination (UN CIMIC) is the function within the military component of a UN peace operation responsible for facilitating liaison and coordination between the military component of the UN mission and its civilian counterparts and partners. In the UN integrated mission context, the military component is one of many UN mission components and functions as part of the overall UN System. As such, it participates in a wide network of coordination mechanisms that, taken together, constitute mission-wide coordination. UN CIMIC is not responsible for all aspects of civil-military coordination, but it has a very specific role to play in the context of mission support and community support, and the overall liaison and information management function required to sustain these two types of military support to civilian partners in a UN peace operations context.

INTRODUCTION

Over the last two decades, the *civil-military coordination* concept has developed on two levels, the strategic level and the operational/tactical level. When it is used at the strategic level, it refers to a type of mission construct, and when used at the operational and tactical level, it refers to a specific function within the military force. These multiple identities and meanings have caused considerable confusion.

At the strategic level, civil-military coordination is used to suggest a multi-dimensional, whole-of-government or comprehensive approach, where various civilian and at least one military entity are engaged

---

Particulars of Original Publication:
Reprinted with permission of the *Journal of Military and Strategic Studies* (Fall, 2007). Available online from <http://www.jmss.org/2007/2007fall/index2.htm>.

in a joint initiative or mission. From the military perspective, it is understandable that all possible missions, for example, United Nations (UN) integrated missions; NATO (North Atlantic Treaty Organization) comprehensive approaches; national PRT-type (Provincial Reconstruction Teams), whole-of-government missions; or African Union (AU) multi-dimensional missions are viewed as military-civilian relationships, because from the military perspective, they all represent some form of military mission that requires them to have a relationship with one or more civilian entities. Peacekeeping used to be a military affair, but more and more civilian roles were added after the end of the Cold War, when UN peace operations started to change from being ceasefire observation operations to becoming multi-dimensional missions meant to support the implementation of comprehensive peace agreements. To reflect the fact that these military operations now had to manage a new type of mission that included civilian entities, these kinds of missions were sometimes referred to in civil-military coordination terms. As the civilian dimension of the post-Cold War peace missions grew in scope and number, however, the bi-polar civil-military concept no longer adequately described the new multi-polar coordination challenges of contemporary UN peace missions. In the UN integrated missions context, for instance, the focus is instead on country-level, system-wide coordination across the political, security, development, rule of law, human rights, and humanitarian dimensions.

The point is that whilst civil-military coordination may thus still be a meaningful term to describe the relationship between a NATO-type military operation and its civilian counterparts at the strategic level, the term is no longer meaningfully applied at the strategic level to UN peace missions, because in these missions, the military component is embedded in a new multi-dimensional reality, where the emphasis has shifted from civil-military coordination to mission-wide coordination in the integrated mission context.

At the operational and tactical levels, civil-military coordination is used to refer to the specific policies, modalities, structures, and tactics that are used to manage the relationship between the military and other components of an operation. At this level, the focus has predominantly been on the humanitarian-military relationship, and two distinct sets of policies have developed over the years: one policy-set that deals with the relationship from a military perspective, that is, NATO Civil-Military Co-operation (CIMIC) doctrine, and another dealing with it from a humanitarian perspective, referred to as UN Humanitarian Civil-Military Coordination (UN CMCoord). Civil-military coordination beyond the humanitarian-military relationship, for instance, in the contexts of disarmament, demobilization, and reintegration (DDR);

security sector reform (SSR); rule of law (RoL); electoral support; etc., has not been adequately dealt with at the operational/tactical level from a policy perspective. In this vacuum, the policies developed for the very specific needs of the humanitarian-military relationship, where the independence of the civilian partners are emphasized and safeguarded, is often misapplied in a peacebuilding context, where there is no need for such emphasis on separate identities and guarded coordination.[1]

This paper focuses on the way the civil-military coordination concept is used in contemporary UN peace operations. It reflects on the civil-military coordination policy debate and places it in the context of contemporary thinking about UN peace operations. The paper deals with civil-military coordination at both the strategic- and operational/tactical-levels in the UN context, it addresses a number of factors that are unique to the UN mission context, and it describes and discusses the operational and tactical manifestations of the civil-military coordination function in contemporary UN missions.

The paper aims to further our understanding of civil-military coordination by clarifying how the concept is understood, shaped, and applied in contemporary UN peace operations. In so doing, those familiar with the concept in other contexts (for instance, in the context of national doctrine, or with the way it is being used in NATO, the European Union [EU], or the AU) should be in a better position to understand the different contexts within which the concept can be understood and applied. This should help avoid or clear-up misunderstandings and contribute to improved coherence and coordination when and where people from these different entities plan and operate together.

Navigating the Conceptual Confusion

When analysing specific civil-military coordination definitions, policies, and doctrines, it should first be noted that these have all been developed for the operational/tactical level. There seem to be two main conceptual streams, that is, co-operation and coordination, and an acronym soup of specific functions and titles: CIMIC, CIMCO, CMO, CMA, CMCoord, CML, CMLO, and so on.

Before we unpack civil-military coordination as it is used in the UN context, it should be noted that there are several other concepts in use outside the UN context, of which Civil-Military Co-operation (CIMIC) – as it is used by NATO,[2] most countries in Europe, as well as Canada, Australia, and New Zealand – is the best known and most widely used. The EU also uses a slightly different CIMIC[3] concept, and is now also developing a new Civil-Military Coordination (CIMCO) concept. The

US has its own terminology and doctrine, and they use the term Civil Military Operations (CMO)[4] to describe their overall concept.

UN peace operations differ from most NATO, EU, and coalition peace and stability operations in that: (a) they are typically consent-based operations, given that they are deployed after a ceasefire or peace agreement has been signed at the request of the parties to the conflict in order to support them with the implementation of the peace agreement, and (b) the military force is deployed as part of an integrated peace mission under overall civilian direction, and in so doing, becomes embedded in the UN mission.

From a UN military perspective, the civil-military relationship between the military component and the other multi-dimensional components of a UN peace operation and between the military component and the rest of the UN System[5] will already be predetermined to a large degree by existing UN policies[6] and by the mandate and organizational structure[7] of the specific UN peace operation. There is thus no need, in the UN context, to motivate for the establishment of mission-specific, civil-military coordination mechanisms to manage this relationship, as there would already be several mission-wide coordination mechanisms built into the mission design[8] and an expectation that further mechanisms will be established as the need arises.

NATO, EU, AU, and coalition-type operations, in contrast, are typically deployed in a more contested environment as stability (peace enforcement) operations, either to secure a ceasefire or to support a ceasefire or peace agreement in situations where there is still considerable hostility by some factions against the peace agreement, as is the case in Afghanistan, Sudan (Darfur), and Somalia in 2007, when this article was written. They are deployed as essentially military operations that exist as a separate legal and organizational entity from the UN or other international or regional groupings that may be active in the conflict-prevention, peacemaking, or peacebuilding spheres in the same country. There is thus a need for these operations to establish liaison and co-operation arrangements between themselves and their civilian counterparts, including with the UN mission and agencies that share the same theatre of operations.

Whilst in many cases such NATO, EU, AU, and coalition operations act under a UN Security Council authority and are thus meant to be part of the international communities' larger strategic comprehensive approach to the conflict in question, the relationship between the military and civilian entities in a UN integrated mission and a NATO-type military mission is fundamentally different. The point is that whilst there is a need to establish strategic-level, civil-military co-operation linkages in NATO-type military operations, no such need exists in the UN integrated mission context, where the military component is embedded in the mission and participates in several mission-wide coordination mechanisms.

The use of co-operation versus coordination is somewhat related to this distinction. From a UN perspective, coordination refers to a spectrum of relations that range from coexistence to co-operation. This UN coordination concept has been developed in the context of humanitarian civil-military coordination, where coexistence refers to a situation where the minimum necessary information is being shared between the humanitarian community and a military combatant force. This would typically include sharing information about security, movement of humanitarian convoys, and the management of shared resources, for example, a port or airport. Co-operation refers to a maximum state of civil-military coordination, where there is a range of co-operative relations between the humanitarian community and a military force that is not regarded as a combatant force, typically including joint planning, division of labour, and sharing of information.[9] The UN and NATO understanding of co-operation and coordination seem to be reversed, because in the NATO context, co-operation is understood to imply a less binding relationship than coordination, and NATO argues that the humanitarian community will be willing to co-operate, but not to coordinate, and they therefore use co-operation.[10]

UN Terminology and Concepts for Civil–Military Coordination

The UN peace operations and humanitarian community has agreed on the common use of the term civil-military coordination. There are, however, several abbreviations and at least two distinct approaches within the UN context.

There are two compatible yet different approaches to civil-military coordination in the UN context, namely a humanitarian and a peace operations approach. The UN Office for the Coordination of Humanitarian Affairs (OCHA) has, under the authority of the Inter-Agency Standing Committee (IASC), facilitated the development of a series of UN humanitarian civil-military coordination policies and guidelines. These include:

- the *Guidelines on the use of Military and Civil Defence Assets in Disaster Relief* (the so-called *Oslo Guidelines,* first adopted in May 1994 and re-launched in 2006);
- the discussion paper and guidelines on the *Use of Military or Armed Escorts for Humanitarian Convoys* of September 2001; and
- the *Guidelines on the Use of Military and Civil Defence Assets to Support United Nations Humanitarian Activities in Complex Emergencies* of March 2004.

In addition, in June 2004, the IASC adopted a reference paper on *Civil-Military Relations in Complex Emergencies* that complements and expands the principles and guidelines previously developed on the use of military and civil defence assets and armed escorts. It also provides guidance of a more general nature for civil-military coordination in humanitarian emergencies.

The complex emergency guidelines and the reference paper also introduced a new concept into our vocabulary, namely UN Humanitarian Civil-Military Coordination (UN CMCoord), which is defined as:

> The essential dialogue and interaction between civilian and military actors in humanitarian emergencies that is necessary to protect and promote humanitarian principles, avoid competition, minimize inconsistency, and when appropriate, pursue common goals. Basic strategies range from coexistence to co-operation. Coordination is a shared responsibility facilitated by liaison and common training.[11]

Taken together, the three humanitarian civil-military coordination guidelines and the reference paper represent the UN policy on humanitarian civil-military coordination.

The UN guidelines for humanitarian-military coordination can be summarized in the following six operating principles for the use of military assets in humanitarian operations:

1. Decisions to accept military assets must be made by humanitarian organizations, not political authorities, and based solely on humanitarian criteria.

2. Military assets should be requested only where there is no comparable civilian alternative and only if the use of military assets can meet a critical humanitarian need. The military asset must therefore be unique in nature or timeliness of deployment, and its use should be as a last resort.

3. A humanitarian operation using military assets must retain its civilian nature and character. The operation must remain under the overall authority and control of the humanitarian organization responsible for that operation, whatever the specific command arrangements for the military asset itself. As much as possible, the military asset should operate unarmed and be civilian in appearance.

4. Countries providing military personnel to support humanitarian operations should ensure that they respect the code of conduct and the principles of the humanitarian organization responsible for that deployment.

5. The large-scale involvement of military personnel in the direct delivery of humanitarian assistance should be avoided.
6. Any use of military assets should ensure that the humanitarian operation retains its international and multi-lateral character.[12]

From a UN peace operations perspective, it is important to understand that these UN humanitarian policies and guidelines for civil-military coordination are focused on, and limited to, the humanitarian dimension of civil-military coordination, that is, between humanitarian actors and the military. Humanitarian actors are those motivated by the humanitarian principles of humanity, impartiality, neutrality, and independence and who act to save lives and alleviate suffering by meeting the people's most basic needs (water, sanitation, health, food, shelter, etc.).

At the operational/tactical level in UN peace operations, civil-military coordination takes place between the military component and all the civilian components of the UN mission, other members of the UN system, and all the other external[13] and internal[14] actors in the mission area. Thus, apart from liaison with the independent (from the UN) humanitarian actors, civil-military coordination in the UN peace operation and peacebuilding context is likely to include interaction with mission civilian functions such as political affairs; civil affairs; public information; human rights; DDR; rule of law and/or judicial affairs; SSR; elections; recovery, rehabilitation and reconstruction; return and resettlement of refugees and IDPs; civil- and child-protection, etc., and the various entities that make up the mission support component, as well as various civilian actors outside the UN mission such as UN agencies, donor agencies, international development NGOs, private contractors, the local civilian authorities, the local civil society, and so on.

The civil-military coordination concept in the UN peace operations context has to cover all possible mission scenarios and has to be relevant to the whole lifespan of a peace operation – from the stabilization phase, which will typically be focused on achieving a safe and secure environment and on providing support to humanitarian action, through the transition and consolidation phases, which will typically be more peacebuilding focused.[15] The point is that civil-military coordination in the UN peace operations context thus has to address a series of relationships and a range of mission scenarios and mission phases which extend beyond the humanitarian dimension.

The UN Department of Peacekeeping Operations (DPKO) has developed a civil-military coordination policy specifically for UN peace operations that was released in September 2002. The DPKO definition of civil-military coordination is as follows:

> UN civil-military coordination is the system of interaction involving exchange of information, negotiation, de-confliction, mutual support, and planning at all levels between military elements and humanitarian organizations, development organizations, and the local civilian population to achieve UN objectives.[16]

Because of the confusion caused by the number of acronyms already in use in the civil-military coordination/co-operation field at that time, the 2002 DPKO policy refrained from using a specific acronym for civil-military coordination. However, in practice, DPKO has been using the abbreviation CIMIC in most of its mission plans, mission structures, and staff appointments to date, with two exceptions. The term CIMCOORD, which has no definitional or policy reference, is currently being used by the military component in the UN Mission in Haiti (MINUSTAH).[17] In the UN Mission in Sudan (UNMIS), the term Civil-Military Liaison Officer (CMLO), which is the term allocated for UN peace operations military personnel in the 2004 IASC reference paper, has been used to describe the staff function, while the branch at headquarters is still being referred to as CIMIC.[18]

At the time of writing, DPKO was considering a revised civil-military coordination policy, and a debate was underway as to whether DPKO should adopt the CMLO terminology proposed for UN peace operations use in the 2004 IASC reference paper or whether is should continue to use CIMIC. Those in favour of the Civil-Military Liaison (CML) terminology argue that the term CIMIC is inappropriate in the UN context because it is generally accepted to refer to interaction that is purely related to the achievement of a military commander's mission.[19]

This article takes a more pragmatic approach based on the recognition that CIMIC, as an acronym, is now so entrenched in the military culture that it would take a disproportional effort to dislodge it. The focus on the CIMIC acronym makes this an unnecessarily confrontational or negative debate. A more pragmatic approach would be to capitalize on the fact that most military officers should be familiar with the CIMIC acronym, and probably understand it broadly to refer to civil-military relations. The DPKO should focus on how CIMIC is different in the UN integrated mission context, rather than on trying to stop the use of the CIMIC acronym. By using UN CIMIC as the acronym for the UN peacekeeping definition of civil-military coordination, DPKO will make it easier for Troop Contributing Countries (TCCs) to merge the UN CIMIC concept with their own national, regional, or alliance CIMIC doctrinal approaches when preparing staff officers and units for service in UN peace operations. It will also make it easier for the UN, the AU, and others to manage transitions between missions, or to work alongside each other, as in the UN/AU hybrid mission in Darfur, or with the EU co-deployments with the UN in the Democratic Republic of the Congo.

UN CIVIL–MILITARY COORDINATION (UN CIMIC) IN PRACTICE

UN civil-military coordination is the function within the military component of a UN peace operation responsible for facilitating liaison and coordination between the military component of the UN mission, other civilian UN mission components, UN agencies,[20] non-UN external actors (including NGOs, etc.), and the host community (including national and local authorities, civil society, traditional and community leaders, etc.). For the sake of using a specific acronym for civil-military coordination as a function within the military component of a UN peace operation at the operational/tactical level, this article will use UN CIMIC.

The primary role of the military component of a UN peace operation is to ensure a safe and secure environment within which the rest of the external and internal actors can operate. A secondary role of the military component is to make its resources available to external and internal actors in support of the overall mission objectives. For instance, in the context of a DDR programme, the military component, over and above its security function, may be in a position to provide transport, medical services, camp building, weapons storage, and/or weapon destruction services to the civilian DDR unit within the mission and the various agencies and actors that support the national DDR coordination mechanism. In such a scenario, the military component is likely to second liaison officers and subject experts to the mission's DDR unit, provide military observers to assist with the verification of combatants and weapons, provide military units to secure the area where DDR activities are being undertaken, provide experts to manage the storage and/or destruction of weapons, provide engineers to assist with camp building and maintenance, etc.

The fact that UN CIMIC is a secondary role within the military component of a UN peace operation is reflected in the scope of the human, financial, and operational resources dedicated to the UN CIMIC function in comparison to those dedicated to the core operational or security function of the military component.

For example, in the UN Mission in Sudan (UNMIS) in 2006, there were ten UN CIMIC staff officers at the Force and Sector Headquarters.[21] Of these, three were at the Force HQ and one each at seven Sector HQs. The total approved force strength for UNMIS in 2006 was approximately 10,000 troops, so the UN CIMIC component represents only 0.001 per cent of the total force strength. Similarly, in the UN Mission in Liberia (UNMIL) in 2007, there were seven UN CIMIC staff officers at Force HQ and one UN CIMIC staff officer at each of the four Sector HQs, that is, eleven UN CIMIC staff officers in total. The UN CIMIC compliment in UNMIL thus represents 0.007 per cent of the approximately 15,000 approved force strength.

The ratios for UNMIS and UNMIL given here are representative of the ratios found in the other contemporary, UN integrated missions. The point is that CIMIC remains a small, specialized staff function that represents a very small percentage of the overall effort of the military component of a UN peace operation.

In all current UN peace operations, the UN CIMIC function is the responsibility of two different types of UN CIMIC officers, namely staff officers and unit-level officers. In UN missions, the UN CIMIC branch consists of staff officers at the Force HQ and Sector HQ levels. At unit level, there are usually liaison officers of some kind, but these are not officially part of the UN CIMIC branch of the mission. In practice, however, the Force HQ and Sector HQ UN CIMIC staff will work closely with the liaison officers at unit level, as that is where most of the UN CIMIC mission support and community support tasks are performed.

At Force HQ, there is typically a small UN CIMIC cell. The Force HQ UN CIMIC cell is usually either a sub-section of the operations branch, or in some cases, it may be a separate command function. In the UN Mission in the Democratic Republic of the Congo (MONUC), for instance, the CIMIC cell is located within a larger operational support branch alongside engineering and medical support. The UN CIMIC HQ cell is usually organized around a UN CIMIC Chief at colonel or lieutenant colonel level, and a Deputy UN CIMIC Chief at lieutenant colonel or major level. The other UN CIMIC staff at Force HQ are usually organized as liaison officers for the sectors as in UNMIL, or around thematic areas, for example, those responsible for dealing with humanitarian agencies (mission support), local authorities (community support), and Quick Impact Projects. A UN CIMIC cell at Force HQ can range from three (UNMIS) to seven (UNMIL), and will rarely be more than ten.

At Sector HQ, there is usually at least one UN CIMIC officer at the rank of major or captain. In some missions, there may be a team of two or more UN CIMIC officers per sector organized around team sites or UN CIMIC houses (UNMEE). The UN CIMIC sector officer serves as the link between the military units and the HQ, maintains sector level UN CIMIC information, and serves as a coordination point between the military component and civilian partners at sector level.

Most military units, which are typically infantry or mechanized infantry battalions but which may also include specialized units such as engineering battalions, transport units, medical hospitals, and air wings, do not deploy into a UN peace operation with a separate UN CIMIC officer. Soon after deployment, however, they realize the need to have some kind of liaison officer who can serve as a focal point for contact with civilian partners. Unfortunately, in most cases, this means that someone who already has a given staff function is tasked to also serve as the UN CIMIC officer. This is typically the second in command, the adjutant to the commander, the intelligence officer, or the military information officer. The latter two options are problematic and are not advisable, as the UN CIMIC function should be seen to be carried out as independently as possible.[22] Even though the liaison officer at unit level may not be appointed as such, we can regard this person as the unit-level UN CIMIC officer for the purposes of this article.

Key UN CIMIC Roles and Functions

One can identify three distinct UN CIMIC functions in UN peace operations, namely liaison and information management, mission support, and community support.[23]

Liaison and information management lies at the core of coordination and refers to a wide range of activities involving the exchange and management of information at all UN CIMIC levels. Depending on where one finds oneself on the coexistence/co-operation spectrum, these activities can include, for example, participating in joint assessments, joint planning, and attending or hosting coordination meetings. In most cases in UN peace operations, UN CIMIC officers will be attending liaison meetings rather than hosting them, as the focus is on liaison with others and not on coordinating others. In some cases (where relevant and needed), UN CIMIC officers may host or provide briefings on the security situation to their civilian partners.

Mission support refers to those actions a military component undertakes in support of an external civilian partner, for instance, providing transport, providing specialized equipment or expertise, or providing a security escort for a humanitarian convoy. The range of activities covered by the mission support function can be divided into two categories, namely the provision of military assets and the provision of security services. As introduced earlier, the UN humanitarian community has developed specific policies and guidelines for the use of military assets on the one hand, and the use of military escorts on the other, and these policies and guidelines are used to steer the role of UN CIMIC mission support in the context of humanitarian-military relations. Most contemporary UN peace operations have a range of peacebuilding mandates as well, and a number of new mission support activities are emerging in the context of, for example, DDR, SSR, and RoL.

Community support refers to those actions military units undertake to support local communities and to build confidence in the peace process. Such actions can include rehabilitating infrastructure such as roads and bridges; supporting social services such as schools and clinics; and supporting national reconciliation and nation-building initiatives such as national and cultural celebrations and sports initiatives. Community support activities can be funded in a variety of ways. A military unit, like any other component within a UN mission, can apply for the use of Quick Impact Projects (QIP).[24] In some cases, UN CIMIC officers will be involved in identifying potential QIP projects, facilitating applications, and supervising and monitoring their execution, but the actual projects will be carried out by local contractors (e.g., school and water point rehabilitation by UNMEE). In others, military units may actually carry out the work, and QIP funds are used to purchase the material (e.g., minor bridge and road rehabilitation by UNAMSIL). In some cases, military units are provided with national funds for UN CIMIC community support projects (e.g., Spain in UNIFIL and Finland in UNMEE) or with medical and other supplies (e.g., Egypt in UNMIS). In yet others, the military units themselves collect funds among the soldiers for community support activities (e.g., Nigeria in UNMIL) or share some of their own stores with the communities where they are deployed (e.g., Pakistan in UNMIL and MONUC). In some cases, a country will deploy specialized personnel with its units with the sole purpose of community support activities (e.g., India with the deployment of a veterinary doctor in UNMIS).

These types of community support projects have the potential to be confused with, or to be wrongly reported as, humanitarian activities, and this is a source of tension within the humanitarian community.[25] It is thus important that military units receive clear guidance as to what are considered appropriate community support activities, and that these be closely coordinated with their civilian counterparts through the UN CIMIC function.[26] It is the responsibility of the force commander, on the advice of his CIMIC staff and in close coordination with the DSRSG/RC/HC, to provide such guidance to the military units serving in a specific mission, and it is the responsibility of the DPKO to provide generic principles and guidance for all UN peace operations.[27]

It is important to note that the work of the UN CIMIC staff officers at Force and Sector Headquarters will focus primarily on liaison and information management. The mission support and community support UN CIMIC activities will typically be carried out by the appropriate tactical military unit that has the requisite resources and expertise. UN CIMIC officers will channel the requests for mission and community support, advise their commanders on the appropriateness of the support, and coordinate among the various stakeholders involved, whilst the actual tactical execution of the mission and community support tasks will be the responsibility of the unit selected and tasked to execute it. In some cases, however, especially at unit level, it cannot be ruled out that the UN CIMIC officer may be tasked to carry out specific UN CIMIC operations, such as commanding a military escort for a humanitarian convoy or supervising a specific community support project such as rehabilitating a local school. Whilst UN CIMIC officers should have received specialized training in UN civil-military coordination policy and practice either prior to deployment or in-mission, it is unlikely that the tactical units executing mission support and community support tasks would have been exposed to such training or policies. It is thus important that the CIMIC officers provide adequate briefings to the tactical units in question and monitor their performance with a view to arranging additional training, where necessary.

UN Integrated Missions and Civil–Military Coordination

The mixed findings of a number of recent peacekeeping, humanitarian, and peacebuilding evaluation reports[28] and related research[29] and the poor sustainability of peacebuilding activities undertaken to date[30] have resulted in a renewed focus on efforts aimed at improving our ability to undertake meaningful, coherent, coordinated, and sustainable peace interventions. For example, the *Joint Utstein Study of Peacebuilding* that analyzed 336 peacebuilding projects implemented by Germany, the Netherlands, the UK, and Norway over the last decade has identified a lack of coherence at the strategic level – what it terms a "strategic deficit" – as the most significant obstacle to sustainable peacebuilding.[31] The Utstein study found that more than 55 per cent of the programmes it evaluated did not show any link to a larger country strategy.

The UN system has responded to this challenge by commissioning a series of high-level panels and working groups[32] to consider various aspects of this dilemma and by experimenting with a number of strategic and operational coordination models.[33] These efforts culminated over the last half-decade in the development of the integrated missions concept. Integrated missions refers to a specific type of operational process and design, where the planning and coordination processes of the different elements of the UN family are integrated into a single, country-level UN System when it undertakes complex peace operations.

The former UN Secretary-General Kofi Annan released a note on integrated missions that describes the concept as follows:

> An integrated mission is based on a common strategic plan and a shared understanding of the priorities and types of programme interventions that need to be undertaken at various stages of the recovery process. Through this integrated process, the UN system seeks to maximize its contribution towards countries emerging from conflict by engaging its different capabilities in a coherent and mutually supportive manner.[34]

The integrated missions concept thus refers to a type of mission where there are processes, mechanisms, and structures in place that generate and sustain a common strategic objective as well as a comprehensive operational approach among the political, security, development, human rights, and where appropriate, humanitarian, UN actors at country level.[35]

The note of the Secretary-General on integrated missions establishes the integrated missions concept as the guiding principle for future complex peace operations. It states that

> [i]ntegration is the guiding principle for the design and implementation of complex UN operations in post-conflict situations and for linking the different dimensions of peacebuilding (political, development, humanitarian, human rights, rule of law, social, and security aspects) into a coherent support strategy.[36]

However, one needs to be mindful that there is at least one other way in which the integrated missions terminology is being used within the UN. The primary usage of the concept, as reflected in the *Note of Guidance on Integrated Missions* released by the UN Secretary-General, refers to *system-wide* integration and is linked to a specific type of mission structure. Through UN General Assembly Resolution 46/182 of 1991, the UN has been given the role of coordinating humanitarian assistance through the Emergency Relief Coordinator internationally, and the Humanitarian Coordinator (HC) system at country level. The UN plays a similar role in development coordination through the UN Development Group (UNDG) and the Resident Coordinator (RC) system at country level. The UN is present in almost all developing countries, and the various UN agencies, funds, and programmes in these countries are coordinated by the RC/HC. In the UN peace operation context, a mission becomes an "integrated mission" when the RC/HC function is integrated with the peace operation through the appointment of a Deputy Special Representative of the Secretary-General (DSRSG/RC/HC). The Secretary-General's note on integrated missions states that it applies to all missions that fall within this category.[37]

The second way in which the integrated missions terminology is being used refers to *multi-dimensional* integration. In this context, it refers to the "integration" of the various military, police, and civilian components of a peace operation in a single office or unit. For instance, when the UN Department of Peacekeeping Operations (DPKO)[38] establishes an integrated mission training cell, it is meant to indicate that the military, police, and civilian training functions in a particular mission have been integrated into a single unit. This use of the terminology is confusing and should rather be replaced with the "Joint" concept, as is used by DPKO when it refers to the "Joint Operations Centre" or the "Joint Mission Analysis Cell."[39]

Integration in the system-wide context of a UN integrated mission is not intended to imply the incorporation of one entity into another, nor is it meant to subsume one entity under the management control (meaning control over resources) and command of another. Each UN department, programme, fund, office, etc., is meant to maintain its own mandate, identity, management system, funding lines, and financial responsibility. Instead, it refers to the processes, mechanisms, and structures that are applied to connect these various UN entities and the peacebuilding dimension within which they carry out their work together into a single interlinked, mutually supportive, comprehensive, UN, country-level System. The objectives of this kind of integration are harmonization, alignment, and coherence with a view to greater overall efficiency and effectiveness. The assumption of the integrated mission concept is thus that a coherent approach that manages to produce a comprehensive and coordinated UN system-wide effort will have a more relevant, effective, efficient, and sustainable impact on the peace process.

Within the UN system, there are various semi-autonomous agencies, funds, offices, and programmes that have a humanitarian and development mandate, as well as departments of the UN Secretariat that are responsible for peace operations. Although the core of the UN integration effort will be aimed at achieving system-wide coherence among these members of the overall UN System, the integration effort is not meant to be exclusively that of the UN. The members within the UN System, and the UN integrated mission specifically, will facilitate and participate in various other coordination initiatives aimed at promoting harmonization among the external actors, and alignment between the internal and external actors in any given country or regional conflict system. In a number of emerging doctrines, including the EU and NATO, this broader strategic coordination process of establishing linkages among all the external actors in a given country or regional conflict system is referred to as the comprehensive approach.

Among some donors, there are also initiatives underway to improve coherence internally among the different government departments engaged in international diplomacy, peace operations, development, and humanitarian assistance. In the UK, this process is known as the so-called joined-up, or whole-of-government approach. In Canada, this initiative was known as the so-called 3D process, as it combined the defence, diplomatic, and development functions of government.

The integrated missions concept should thus be understood in a wider international context where coherence[40] is being pursued at the national level among government departments and internationally among donors (harmonization[41]); between donor and recipients (alignment[42]);

within the UN development, humanitarian, and environment dimensions (system-wide coherence[43]); between the peace, security, human rights, humanitarian, and development dimensions of the UN System at country level (system-wide integration); and among the military, police, and civilian components of a UN peace operation (multi-dimensional integration).

The integrated mission concept has now been officially accepted in the UN System as the mission structure of choice.[44] It will be the dominant management structure for UN complex peace operations in the near- to mid-term, and it is likely that the EU, the AU,[45] and others will try to apply its core features to their own future missions. However, one needs to be mindful that integration in a non-UN context will necessarily refer to multi-dimensional integration, rather than system-wide integration. For instance, the AU's Integrated Planning Task Force (IPTF) refers to a mechanism where the military, police, and civilian planning functions are combined into one process,[46] as opposed to the UN integrated mission (IMTF) that refers to the coming together of planners from the UN Department of Peacekeeping Operations (DPKO), UN Department of Political Affairs (DPA), UN Development Group, UN Office for the Coordination of Humanitarian Affairs (OCHA), and others in the UN system. Non-UN entities such as NATO, the EU, or the AU would not be able to achieve the same degree of integration with UN development and humanitarian agencies that is possible for a UN peace operation simply because the former is not part of the UN and cannot therefore be part of the UN System. That does not imply, however, that it is not possible to achieve meaningful coherence and coordination between entities like NATO and the AU on the one hand, and UN system agencies on the other. It only means that the integrated missions terminology cannot be meaningfully applied when the coherence and coordination being pursued goes beyond the UN System.

Practical Challenges for the UN Integrated Missions Approach

As with any new innovation, the integrated mission concept has not been without its detractors, and it has highlighted various technical, administrative, organizational, and budgetary challenges that need to be overcome before all aspects of the model can be fully implemented. The most serious concerns raised to date relate to the perceived loss of humanitarian independence when the Humanitarian Coordinator (HC) becomes one of the Deputy Special Representatives of the Secretary-General (DSRSG). Whilst most humanitarian UN agencies seem to feel that by becoming part of the UN integrated mission structure they have more opportunities to influence the direction of the mission and to protect humanitarian space, more independent-minded humanitarian NGOs have opted to create their own humanitarian coordination mechanisms that are more loosely connected to the HC function than before. This seems to be more acute in situations where OCHA has withdrawn or where the humanitarian coordination function has been incorporated into the UN mission, for example, in UNMIL/Liberia.

There is also a more generally held view, however, that the integrated mission concept will make it more difficult for individual agencies to be associated with their products, and therefore to raise funds on the basis of their perceived visibility in a particular crisis. For instance, whilst a multitude of UN and non-UN agencies have worked together in the DDR campaign in Liberia and are still working together in Sudan, the overall effects are generally reported as, and perceived to be, UN mission achievements. Whilst the UN integrated mission has been accepted as the mission structure of choice at the highest levels within member states, the UN secretariat, and the UN agencies, these problems at country level still bedevil its acceptance at the operational level. The degree of resistance to, and frustration with, the integrated mission model at the country level is itself causing dysfunction and has resulted in the implementation of the concept having unintended consequences.

THE ROLE OF UN CIMIC IN MISSION-WIDE COORDINATION

The UN integrated mission concept has a number of important implications for UN CIMIC. Firstly, it firmly embeds the military component of the UN peace operation within the larger, system-wide functions of the UN System. This moves us away from the structural approach where we previously referred to military and civilian components, and thus moves civil-military coordination to a new functional or dimensional vocabulary where we talk about the integration of dimensions such as security, political, human rights, rule of law, humanitarian, and development. Within this conceptualization, *security* is not equal to *military,* as it could contain a number of functions, such as security sector reform, demining, public order, and so on that are not necessarily the responsibility of the military component of the UN peace operation. Nor is the utility and contribution of the military component limited to the security dimension, as they can contribute to the achievement of objectives in the other dimensions in a wide variety of ways, both through their primary security role (civil protection, etc.) and their secondary roles, including UN CIMIC (making military assets available to achieve or support humanitarian, developmental, RoL, SSR, political objectives, etc. or through direct community support activities).

In order to assess, plan, coordinate, and monitor the roles and responsibilities of all the various actors so as to achieve and maintain momentum across the UN System and between the UN System and other internal and external actors, a new type of coordination is necessary. The civil-military coordination concept is no longer adequate to describe this level of system-wide coordination. Within the UN integrated mission, there is now a range of coordination systems that are interlinked and that provide a network of coordination processes; these, when taken together, represent the mission coordination system. Civil-military coordination in the form of UN CIMIC – that is, the function of coordinating between the military component and other civilian partners in the context of mission and community support – is one of the instruments of mission coordination. Others include processes such as the senior management team, security management system, logistical coordination systems, the joint operations centre (JOC), the integrated missions planning process (IMPP), the joint analysis centre (JMAC), and so on.

The point is that although civil-military coordination has not been used as an overall operational level coordination tool, the concept has often been used in the past to suggest multi-dimensional cohesion and coordination. The UN integrated mission concept has now developed sufficient momentum to dislodge that kind of misapplied use of the civil-military coordination concept at the strategic level and replaced it with a new understanding of the need for mission coordination: a loose network of a number of specialized or functional coordination mechanisms that, once sufficiently connected, provide an overall mission-wide coordination system.

Blurred Lines between Military versus Civilian Mission Assets

Civil-military coordination essentially deals with two aspects of military support to civilians: the provision of either security (a military escort for a humanitarian convoy, for example), or of military assets like skills, knowledge, and manpower (for example, equipment such as trucks or helicopters and/or skills and knowledge such as medical and engineering expertise). The existing body of humanitarian civil-military coordination policies and guidelines introduced earlier deal with these two areas of military support. A key difference between UN and non-UN missions is, however, the confusion that arises as to what constitutes a military asset in a UN peace operation. On one end of the spectrum, equipment is owned by a troop-contributing country (TCC) and deployed into a UN mission; on the other, equipment is owned by the UN. One problem is that there is no visual distinction between the two in most cases; they are all painted white with black UN markings. Equipment that is obviously military such as an APC or an attack helicopter is probably less problematic, but transport trucks and general purpose helicopters, engineering equipment, and so on are more difficult to identify as military or civilian. In some situations, you may have a UN-owned (civilian) asset like a commercially chartered transport helicopter being used for military tactical purposes such as placing or extracting soldiers into an operational, or even a combat, situation, as in eastern DRC where the UN mission (MONUC) is engaged in collaborative offensive operations.[47] From the perspective of a humanitarian actor, or of the local civilian community, or even of the soldiers in question, it is thus not necessarily obvious in a UN peace operation context whether a specific UN asset is a civilian or military asset, and that makes the application of the UN humanitarian civil-military coordination guidelines regarding this distinction problematic.

One can further complicate the issue by arguing that all UN peace operation assets are in fact operated under a political-security-strategic mandate issued by the UN Security Council and can thus, for the purposes of the humanitarian civil-military policies and guidelines, be regarded as military assets in that they are not neutral and impartial in the way that humanitarian actors would use these concepts. According to this line of reasoning, there are thus, from a humanitarian perspective, no "civilian" assets or personnel in UN peace operations. The issue becomes even further complicated, however, in the UN integrated missions context, where the security and coordination systems of the UN humanitarian and development agencies and that of the UN peace operation, including the military component, are integrated.

The point is that it is not possible to arrive at a clear distinction between military and civilian assets in the UN peace operations context, and even less so in the case of UN integrated missions. Both the UN peace operation community and the humanitarian community, including the UN humanitarian community, should give careful thought to how to maintain the principles of humanitarian independence, neutrality, and impartiality without getting caught up in debates regarding whether a specific piece of UN equipment is military or civilian.

This confusion creates an opportunity to re-focus on the intent of the humanitarian principles instead of getting caught up in trying to apply outdated military and civilian identities. The distinction becomes irrelevant if its use will not have an impact on the perceived neutrality and impartiality of the humanitarian actor. And whenever the use of a UN asset will have an impact on the perceived neutrality and impartiality of a humanitarian actor or cause a security risk for the intended beneficiaries or humanitarian workers in some other fashion, it should not be used.

Civil–Military Coordination outside UN CIMIC

It is also important to remind ourselves that whilst UN CIMIC, in its rightful context within a UN peace operation (including UN integrated missions), is responsible for facilitating liaison and coordination between the military component and other civilian actors, this coordination is limited to the mission- and community-support functions introduced above. In other words, UN CIMIC is not responsible for all potential civil-military coordination roles in a UN peace operation context. There are many areas in which liaison takes place between the military component and other civilian actors that are not channelled through the UN CIMIC function. These include, amongst others, functions such as these:

- military support to UN Security (security of UN personnel and assets) that are coordinated between the military component and the UN mission and UN Country Team security units in coordination with the UN Department of Safety and Security (DSS);
- military support to UN civilian protection objectives that are coordinated by the DSRSG/RC/HC and the force commander, and in some missions, through a system of Protection Working Groups;
- military participation in mission planning that are coordinated through the Integrated Mission Planning Team (IMPT);
- military participation in conflict and situational analysis that are coordinated through the Joint Mission Analysis Centre (JMAC);
- military participation in day-to-day, mission-wide operational coordination that is coordinated through the Joint Operations Centre; and
- military support to UN logistics that requires the close coordination and integration of military logisticians and those within the mission support component, etc.

The point is that UN CIMIC should be understood within the context of its liaison function in the areas of mission support and community support. It should not be misunderstood as a gatekeeper for all civil-military coordination and liaison.

Conclusion

This paper focused on how the civil-military coordination concept is being used in the context of contemporary UN peace operations. It reflected on the policy and doctrinal debates and developments in the field of civil-military coordination at both the strategic and the operational/tactical levels.

The argument was made that the bi-polar civil-military coordination concept at the strategic level no longer adequately describes the system-wide coordination needs of contemporary UN peace operations in the context of the UN integrated mission model. The civil-military coordination concept is still appropriate and meaningful at the operational and tactical levels, both from a humanitarian (UN CMCoord) and a military (UN CIMIC) perspective, but it is important to understand how operational and tactical civil-military coordination is unique in UN peace operations, especially in the integrated missions context.

UN civil-military coordination (UN CIMIC) is the function within the military component of a UN peace operation responsible for facilitating liaison and coordination between the military component of the UN mission and its civilian counterparts and partners. In the UN peace operations context, the military component is one of many UN mission components and functions as part of the overall UN System in the UN integrated missions context. As such, it participates in a wide network of coordination mechanisms that, taken together, constitute mission-wide coordination.

UN CIMIC is one of the elements in the wider coordination network that contributes to overall or system-wide coordination. It is not responsible for all aspects of civil-military coordination, but it has a very specific and important role to play in the context of mission support and community support, and the overall liaison and information management function required to sustain these two types of military support to civilian partners in a UN peace operations context.

The point is that civil-military coordination, within its rightful place at the operational and tactical levels in the UN peace operation context, does have a meaningful role to play in the management of civil-military relations. However, it is important to understand the particular dynamics that will influence the scope of civil-military coordination in the UN integrated mission context and the role of the military component of the UN peace operation, and thus UN CIMIC, within the larger UN System.

NOTES

1. For a discussion on the need to develop civil-military coordination policies for the peacebuilding context, see Cedric de Coning, "Civil-Military Coordination and UN Peacebuilding Operations," in *International Peacekeeping: The Yearbook of International Peace Operations*, Volume 11, ed. H. Langholtz, B. Kondoch, and A. Wells, (Bruxelles: Koninklijke Brill N.V., 2007).
2. The NATO definition of civil-military co-operation (CIMIC) is the coordination and co-operation, in support of the mission, between the NATO commander and civil populations, including national and local authorities

as well as international, national, and non-governmental organizations and agencies. See *Military Policy on Civil-Military Co-operation (CIMIC)*, CIMICWG 001-00, WP(MC411) (NATO: Brussels, 2000), 1.

3. The EU definition of civil-military co-operation (CIMIC) is the coordination and co-operation, in support of the mission, between military components of EU-led Crisis Management Operations and civil role-players (external to the EU), including national population and local authorities, as well as international, national, and non-governmental organizations and agencies. See *Civil-Military Co-operation* (Brussels: EU, 2002), 9.

4. CMO is the activities of a commander that establish, maintain, influence, or exploit relations between military forces, governmental and non-governmental civilian organizations and authorities, and the civilian populace in a friendly, neutral, or hostile operational area in order to facilitate those military operations that consolidate and achieve operational US objectives. Civil-military operations may include performance by military forces of activities and functions normally the responsibility of the local, regional, or national government. These activities may occur prior to, during, or subsequent to other military actions. They may also occur, if directed, in the absence of other military operations. Civil-military operations may be performed by designated civil affairs, by other military forces, or by a combination of civil affairs and other forces. See the following US military publications: JP 3-57, FM 41-10, and JP 1-02.

5. In this paper, "UN system" (not capitalized) is used to refer to all the members of the UN family in a general sense, whilst "UN System" (capitalized) is used in the context of a UN integrated mission where there is a systematic effort to achieve system-wide coherence through various policies, procedures, mechanisms, and processes.

6. See, for instance, the UN Administrative Committee on Coordination's (ACC) *Guidelines on the Functioning of the Resident Coordinator System,* 24 Sept. 1999; the UN Secretary-General's *Note of Guidance on Relations between Representatives of the Secretary-General, Resident Coordinator, and Humanitarian Coordinators,* dated 11 Dec. 2000; the UN Secretary-General's *Note of Guidance on Integrated Missions,* dated 17 Jan. 2006; and the UN Department of Peacekeeping Operations (DPKO)'s *Policy Directive on Joint Operations Centers and Joint Mission Analysis Centers*, dated 31 May 2006.

7. See, for instance, the different types of integrated missions (separate, partial, and fully integrated) identified in *Report on Integrated Missions: Practical Perspectives and Recommendations,* ed. E. Barth Eide, A.T. Kaspersen, R. Kent, and K. von Hippel, (Oslo: Norwegian Institute of International Affairs [NUPI], 2005), 9.

8. Such as the Joint Operations Centre (JOC), the Joint Mission Analysis Cell (JMAC), the Integrated Mission Planning Team (IMPT), etc.

9. OCHA, *Guidelines on the Use of Military and Civil Defence Assets to Support United Nations Humanitarian Activities in Complex Emergencies* (Geneva: UN Office for the Coordination of Humanitarian Affairs [OCHA], 2004), 5.

10. NATO, *Military Policy on Civil-Military Co-operation (CIMIC)*, n. 2.
11. OCHA, *Guidelines on the Use of Military and Civil Defence Assets*, n. 8.
12. These six general operating principles for the use of military assets in support of humanitarian operations were adopted when the *Report of the Task Force on the Use of Military and Civil Defence Assets in Support of Humanitarian Operations* was approved at the nineteenth meeting of the Inter-Agency Standing Committee Working Group on 27 Sept. 1995 in Geneva.
13. External actors are all international actors engaged in undertaking humanitarian assistance, conflict prevention, and peacebuilding activities in a given country or conflict system.
14. Internal actors are all local actors in the country or conflict system where peacebuilding activities take place.
15. For more information on the phases (stabilization, transition, and consolidation) referred to here, see de Coning, n. 1.
16. DPKO, *Policy on Civil-Military Coordination* (New York: UN Department of Peacekeeping Operations, 2002), 2.
17. The exact history behind the use of "CIMCOORD" in MINUSTAH is unclear, but it would seem as if there used to be a civilian OCHA "UN CMCoord" post that was incorporated into the DPKO mission at some point and became "CIMCOORD" in the process. The military component used to have a CIMIC branch, but at some point in the mission's history, the civilian CIMCOORD position was not renewed, and the military took over the CIMCOORD designation.
18. At the time UNMIS was established, DPKO had already developed the first drafts of its new civil-military liaison and coordination policy. While the Force Generation Service of DPKO planned and structured the Force Headquarters with a CIMIC branch, the OCHA CMCoord Officer on the ground convinced the mission that it should adopt the CMLO terminology reserved for peace operations in the 2004 IASC reference paper and in the draft DPKO policy.
19. DPKO, *Civil-Military Liaison in UN Integrated Missions*, final draft, version 8, (New York: UN Department of Peacekeeping Operations, 2007), 4.
20. For ease of reference, "UN agencies" is used here in the generic sense to cover all UN agencies, funds, programmes, and departments.
21. As referred to earlier, in UNMIS these staff officers have been designated as "Civil-Military Liaison Officers (CMLOs)," the terminology identified for UN peace operations in the 2004 IASC reference paper.
22. An intelligence officer who is doubly hated as a CIMIC officer will tend to use his/her CIMIC role as a cover to gather intelligence, and this is likely to cause tension between the unit and humanitarian counterparts. The same would be true for military information officers who would tend to use their CIMIC role as a vehicle for psychological operations as opposed to an end in itself.
23. Cedric de Coning, "Civil-Military Coordination and UN Peacebuilding Operations," African Centre for the Constructive Resolution of Disputes

(ACCORD), *Durban Accord*, 119–45, 2007, <http://jha.ac/articles/a183.pdf>; "CIMIC in UN and African Peace Operations," *Durban Accord*, ed. C. de Coning, 189–216, 2006, <http://www.accord.org.za/cimic/manual.htm>.

24. See DPKO's *Policy Directive on Quick Impact Projects (QIPs)*, 12 Feb. 2007.

25. Stuart Gordon, "Unintended Consequences of Civil-Military Cooperation in Peace Operations," in *The Unintended Consequences of Peacekeeping Operations*, ed. C. Aoi, C. de Coning, and R. Thakur, 109–30, (Tokyo: UN University Press, 2007).

26. See the *Report of the Office of Internal Oversight Services on the Review of Military Involvement in Civil Assistance in Peacekeeping Operations*, dated 13 Dec. 2005.

27. Paragraph 12 of the Secretary-General's *Note of Guidance on Integrated Missions*, dated 17 Jan. 2006, deals with the potential for tension between military hearts-and-minds-type actions and humanitarian assistance, and states that such military actions need to be coordinated with the Deputy Special Representative of the Secretary-General (SRSG) Resident Coordinator/Humanitarian Coordinator (RC/HC).

28. Amongst others: N. Dahrendorf, *A Review of Peace Operations: A Case for Change* (London: King's College, 2003); T. Porter, *An External Review of the CAP* (New York: UN OCHA, 2002); Marc Sommers, *The Dynamics of Coordination*: Occasional Paper no. 40 (Providence: Thomas J. Watson Jr. Institute of International Affairs, 2000); N. Stockton, *Strategic Coordination in Afghanistan* (Kabul: Afghanistan Research and Evaluation Unit [AREU], 2000); and A. Domini, *The Policies of Mercy: UN Coordination in Afghanistan, Mozambique and Rwanda* (Providence: Thomas J. Watson Jr. Institute for International Studies, 2002).

29. For instance, *Ending Civil Wars: The Implementation of Peace Agreements,* ed. S.J. Stedman, E. Cousens, and D. Rothchild, (Boulder: Lynne Rienner, 2002); S. Chesterman, *You, the People: The United Nations, Transitional Administration, and State-Building* (Oxford: Oxford University Press, 2004); F. Fukuyama, *State-Building: Governance and World Order in the 21st Century* (Ithaca: Cornell University Press, 2004); and R. Paris, *At War's End: Building Peace after Civil Conflict* (Cambridge: Cambridge University Press, 2004).

30. See Paul Collier et al., *Breaking the Conflict Trap: Civil War and Development Policy* (New York: Oxford University Press and the World Bank, 2003) and R. Licklider, "The Consequences of Negotiated Settlements in Civil Wars 1945–93," *American Political Science Review* 89, no. 3 (1995): 681–90.

31. Dan Smith, *Towards a Strategic Framework for Peacebuilding: The Synthesis Report of the Joint Utstein Study on Peacebuilding* (Oslo: International Peace Research Institute (PRIO), 2003), 16.

32. See, for instance, the 2005, *In Larger Freedom: Towards Security, Development and Human Rights for All*, Report of the Secretary-General of the UN, <www.un.org/largerfreedom> and the report of the Secretary-General's High-Level Panel on System-Wide Coherence, *Delivering as One* (New York: UN Press, 2006), <www.un.org/events/panel>.

33. For example, the Integrated Mission Task Force concept for mission planning, the Strategic Framework concept in Afghanistan, and the Results Focused Transitional Framework (RFTF) in Sierra Leone.

34. UN, *Note of Guidance on Integrated Missions,* issued by the Secretary-General on 9 Dec. 2005, para. 4. See also the *Revised Note of Guidance on Integrated Missions*, dated 17 Jan. 2006 and released as a note from the Secretary-General on 9 Feb. 2006, para. 4.

35. UN, Integrated Missions Planning Process (IMPP) Guidelines endorsed by the Secretary-General on 13 June 2006, p. 3.

36. *Note of Guidance on Integrated Missions,* n. 25, para. 4.

37. "This updated Note of Guidance applies to all integrated missions in which the SRSG is supported by an RC and HC serving as the Deputy Special Representative of the Secretary-General (DSRSG/RC/HC)." *Note of Guidance on Integrated Missions,* n. 25, para. 3.

38. Note that as of 1 Jan. 2008, DPKO will be split into two departments, namely the Department of Peace Operations (DPO) and the Department of Field Support (DFS). Ref General Assembly Resolution A/RES/61/256 of 22 Mar. 2007.

39. For DPKO's Policy Directive on Joint Operations Centres and Joint Mission Analysis Centres, see n. 6. Although "joint" has a specific meaning in the military context, e.g., a joint army, air force, and navy HQ, it can easily be understood to convey a broader, common sense meaning – parts that previously operated separately are now joined together.

40. See Robert Picciotto, *Fostering Development in a Global Economy: A Whole of Government Perspective, Introduction: Key Concepts, Central Issues* (Paris: OECD, 2005), 13–14, where he identifies: (1) internal coherence, (2) whole-of-government coherence, (3) donor coherence, and (4) country-level coherence.

41. See the *Rome Declaration on Harmonization* of 25 Feb. 2003, <www.aidharmonization.org> [12 May 2007].

42. Note in this context the *Paris Declaration on Aid Effectiveness* of 2 Mar. 2005, <www.oecd.org> [12 May 2007].

43. See the 2006 *Delivering as One* report.

44. *Note of Guidance on Integrated Missions,* n. 29, para. 4.

45. The AU has embarked on an initiative to develop an African Standby Force (ASF) in May 2003 when the first *ASF Policy Framework* was adopted by the third meeting of the African Chiefs of Defence Staff, and endorsed by the Maputo Summit in July 2003. The concept has subsequently been further developed through a series of workshops in 2005 and 2006 that looked at doctrine; training and evaluation; logistics; standing operating procedures; and command, control, and communications. The target date for the operationalization of the ASF is 2010. In the meantime, the AU is engaged in peace operations in Darfur (AMIS) and Somalia (AMISOM),

and both reflect elements of the multi-dimensional approach to integration. For instance, the strategic headquarters of the AMIS mission is the Darfur Integrated Task Force (DITF); it consists of various AU military, police, and civilian planners and support staff, as well as UN, EU, and NATO advisors. The new proposed hybrid AU/UN mission in Darfur would also be an interesting experiment in that it may attempt to combine elements of the system-wide and multi-dimensional approaches to integration.

46. *Draft Policy Framework for the Civilian Dimension of the African Standby Force* (Addis Ababa: AU Peace Support Operations Division [PSOD], 2006), 7.

47. Cedric de Coning, *Peace Operations in Africa: The Next Decade,* Working paper no. 721-2007, July 2007, Oslo, NUPI), 8.

Interagency and Civil-Military Coordination: Lessons from a Survey of Afghanistan and Liberia

Lara Olson and Hrach Gregorian

ABSTRACT

This article examines the gap between today's strong policy consensus on the need for greater coordination in war to peace transitions and the poor results of such coordination efforts in the field. It begins by reviewing the current debates around the coordination challenge and the political and organizational factors that render integration and collaboration problematic between diverse civilian and military assistance agencies. The article then summarizes the main insights from an international practitioner workshop on coordination experiences in Afghanistan and Liberia, identifying blocks and supports to coordination evident in both settings as well as key practical and conceptual challenges, and then suggesting spheres for improvement in existing coordination processes.

WAR TO PEACE TRANSITIONS IN THE POST–COLD WAR ERA

The end of the Cold War brought a dramatic increase in conflicts within states and a similar increase in international peace operations, as complex multi-actor interventions to end civil wars and build peace have come to be known. While in 1998 the United Nations (UN) deployed 14,000 peacekeepers worldwide, today over 90,000 military and civilians are in the field in sixteen UN missions.[1] New international *coalitions of the willing* led by regional organizations like NATO in Kosovo emerged in place of UN involvement in some contexts. More fundamentally, the nature of UN involvement expanded dramatically from classical peacekeeping characterized by the monitoring of ceasefires. New expanded UN missions involved solidifying fragile truces, building the capacity and legitimacy of states emerging from conflict, holding elections, demobilizing and reintegrating combatants, and sometimes, directly administering a territory for a period. As Michael Lund has effectively captured, these changes encompassed a broadening of the goals and sectors that were involved, a deepening of the engagement with the internal workings of societies, and a lengthening of the stages of conflict

---

Particulars of Original Publication:
Reprinted with permission of the *Journal of Military and Strategic Studies* (Fall, 2007). Available online from <http://www.jmss.org/2007/2007fall/index.htm>.

when such missions would be deployed, with preventive and post-conflict state-building missions becoming a major new focus.[2]

A parallel development was a dramatic increase in involvement in these internal conflicts by non-governmental organizations – particularly humanitarian, relief, and development NGOs – to address civilian needs, accompanied by an increase among human rights organizations and conflict resolution groups conducting Track Two negotiation efforts and civil society dialogues across conflict lines. These changes occurred alongside the new ability of the international media to bring the plight of civilians caught in war to the world stage, thereby mobilizing populations in donor countries to push for action.

As a result of these shifts, international efforts to secure peace in conflicts such as Kosovo, East Timor, the Democratic Republic of the Congo (DRC), Haiti, Sierra Leone, Liberia, Afghanistan, Burundi, and Sudan have witnessed the involvement of a dizzying array of actors: foreign diplomats and UN personnel, international military forces, international humanitarian and development agencies and NGOs, and a myriad of national NGOs and civil society groups. A wide range of efforts to promote security, relief, development, peacemaking among leaders, support to civil society, gender equity, mine clearance, and community-level peacebuilding have been undertaken by these actors in the attempt to end violence and build sustainable peace. This spectrum of activities has come to be called *peacebuilding*, often widely (and loosely) defined as all efforts and programs conducted by international and national actors in all sectors and at all levels to solidify peace.[3]

With the added complexity of such international peace missions and the expanded number of international actors and approaches involved, the question of coordination has become a key focus for donors, the UN, other multi-lateral agencies, and NGOs. In numerous reviews of the crises of the 1990s in Mozambique, Angola, Guatemala, Bosnia, and Sierra Leone, problems of coordination amongst the multiplicity of actors were constantly raised. While the critiques were leveled at the UN, the World Bank, other intergovernmental organizations, and donor governments, NGOs were often singled out as especially "anarchic," given their sheer numbers, diversity, and culture of independence.

The trend in peacebuilding since Kosovo in 1999 is towards greater integration of international efforts and the necessity for collaboration between relief, development, and security organizations. By the late 1990s, from key donor countries to UN agencies to NGO networks, a common understanding emerged that efforts for peace must become more strategic and coordinated if they are to have the ambitious impacts they intend. This consensus has led to efforts in recent years to promote explicit communication, coordination, and even formal integration among interveners to achieve greater impact.

Since the late 1990s, this push for more unified efforts has led to such innovations as UN Integrated Missions, which combined the political, peacekeeping, and humanitarian arms of the UN system under a unified command. Indeed, many donor countries have now synchronized the foreign assistance arms of government in what has been variously called the "joined up approach," the "whole of government approach," or the "3-D" approach (referring to defense, development, and diplomacy). The goal has been to use military, political, and humanitarian/development instruments in a more synchronized and presumably more effective manner to achieve security, development, and peace in conflict-affected countries.

CIVIL–MILITARY COORDINATION IN INTERNATIONAL PEACE OPERATIONS

The area of civil-military coordination in the field is even more difficult than other interagency relationships given fundamental differences between international military forces and humanitarian and development agencies in terms of their agendas, operating styles, roles, and the principles and doctrines guiding their work. For groups that do try to engage across these divides, there is often a strong sense of frustration on both sides with the energy invested in trying to establish good communication and clear understanding of each other's positions. Another key issue is that field-level coordination is vulnerable to directives coming from the policy level and to a reported lack of two-way information flow between the field and policy levels. As one NGO representative interviewed commented, "even when military-NGO meetings in the field are quite helpful, and there is lots of mutual respect, in the end things don't change correspondingly, or a new policy comes down from above and there is a sense that the right people were not in the room." [4] Furthermore, field co-operation often depends on developing good personal relationships, but with frequent turnover of personnel, such relationship building must begin from scratch.

In situations of an incomplete or fragile peace, the interlinked nature of security and development is inescapable, with security necessary to enable progress on development, and immediate relief and longer-term development gains necessary to solidify the peace by giving people a stake in the new stability. Roles and mandates often overlap as military forces engage in aid provision and governance support, major donor representatives work directly with provincial and local governments, and development actors participate in the security sector reform spectrum (of DDR, justice reform, and police reform). Whether international military forces, UN and donor country diplomats, and humanitarian and relief agencies choose to explicitly work together or not, the outcomes of their efforts in such settings are deeply intertwined.

Given this interdependence, improving how security and development actors interact in such settings is critical to increasing the probability that their independent efforts will lead to positive outcomes and to increasing the chances that some level of constructive coordination may be developed.

FACTORS CONTRIBUTING TO THE COORDINATION PROBLEM

Many factors render integration and collaboration problematic between diverse assistance agencies, especially between civilian and military agencies. In the discussion below we examine some of these factors, roughly grouped as political and organizational factors.

POLITICAL FACTORS

National Interests and Political Factors

The bilateral engagement of key aid donors in conflict-affected states is often driven by politics more than by technical assessments of need. Commentators note that whole-of-government approaches often tend to be motivated by "classical national interest calculations, based on considerations such as strategic location, diplomatic implications, and economic consequences, as well as intangible variables like colonial history and Diaspora linkages…" [5] Multi-lateral engagement in humanitarian and development activity can also be problematic. The work of UN departments that have sought to step up the level and scope of humanitarian intervention has met with resistance among some in the General Assembly who view such penetration as a threat to state sovereignty.[6] Regional, governmental, and NGO actors all have vested interests that an often vague commitment to multi-lateralism in peacebuilding cannot overcome. Necla Tschirgi of the National Peace Academy writes:

> The integrated policies promoted by the United Nations or the linked-up policies by key donor countries applied primarily to conflicts that did not affect the vital interests of powerful external actors. In politically difficult cases like Kashmir, North Korea, or Palestine, there was little insistence on integrated policies; in other cases like Bosnia, Kosovo and the Democratic Republic of Congo (DRC), the sequencing of security and development approaches decidedly reflected the vital interests of key players.[7]

Tschirgi reminds us that, when advocating for integrated policies, we must ask, Whose security is at stake? Whose development is affected? and Whose agenda has precedence? National governments in conflict-ridden states also worry about being overwhelmed by a range of external actors with differing missions and objectives determined as often by the agency's organizational capacity as the recipient country's needs. Such countries are wary of highly coordinated, multi-donor interventions and the potential threat posed by a "donor cartel." [8]

Incompatible Objectives

Different organizations hold differing, and sometimes mutually contradictory, policy goals. Humanitarian and development agencies are concerned that their core objectives, such as relief, reconstruction, and structural reform, will be subordinated to more immediate security and political concerns. Such incompatibilities can exist within the same organization. One study points to the Organization for Security and Co-operation in Europe (OSCE), "where the democratization branch generally seeks to develop working relationships with local authorities, while the human rights branch is tasked with responding to complaints against local authorities." [9] According to a study of the Liberia case, "Many NGOs in Liberia were unhappy with UNMIL's incorporation of the Humanitarian Coordinator role (as a dual function of the Special Representative of the Secretary-General [SRSG]) as well as the Office for the Coordination of Humanitarian Affairs (OCHA) into the integrated mission framework." The same study quotes the following observation by the International Council of Volunteer Agencies regarding the integrated mission framework in Liberia:

> This step, which could be seen as the final step in realizing the full integration of humanitarian coordination under a political banner, may involve humanitarian concerns becoming subservient to the political process and/or the UN neglecting immediate humanitarian needs. The coordination of humanitarian action needs, however, its own humanitarian space.[10]

As a practical matter, carving out such space is difficult at best. While military units generally undertake UN Civil-Military Coordination (CIMIC) operations according to the national doctrines of their respective nations, these doctrines are not necessarily designed to comport with the specific requirements of humanitarian action in a specific geographic space. Peace operations are most often carried out by the military at the battalion level. Currently, the countries providing the largest number of battalions include Bangladesh, Ethiopia, Ghana, Kenya, Nigeria, Pakistan, South Africa, Ukraine, and Uruguay. According to one study, "none of these countries have a national CIMIC doctrine for use in peace operations." Their soldiers are trained for the most part in counter insurgency warfare, which some are called on to wage in select theaters. As the same study concludes, "without a conscious effort to provide them with clear policies and guidelines for UN CIMIC actions in the UN peace operations where they are deployed, it is natural that they will revert to what they know best, i.e., counter-insurgency style, 'winning hearts and minds' campaigns." [11]

Conflicting Definitions of Peace

The challenge to cross-sectoral collaboration in peacebuilding at the most fundamental level may well come down to differing concepts about the path to, and the ultimate meaning of, peace. Differing conceptions of peace lead to differing approaches to achieving it. Generally speaking, the role of the military has been to achieve peace by winning wars. What some characterize as "mission creep" has expanded this role to include conflict prevention and management in more complex intrastate environments where civil conflict has led to something less than victory or defeat for belligerents who continue to occupy the same physical space. The absence of violence (or negative peace) in such situations is an acceptable end state for military interveners. This may also be characterized as attainment of peace at the symptomatic level; that is, the reduction or elimination of actual (or kinetic) violence. It does not, nor is it designed to, address the underlying or structural causes of violent conflict.

While humanitarian action is generally not concerned with peace but with alleviating immediate suffering, development policy is much more in line with concepts of positive peace, which includes attempts to root out and ameliorate the causes of conflict in state and society. The requirements of positive peace are complex and vary depending on the socio-economic and political characteristics of a given society. Addressing these factors is usually believed to be a long-term proposition, requiring sustained programming across a range of activities planned and executed with maximum input from key actors in the host nation. In theory, structural change will lead to transformation in human relations leading to stable and sustainable peace that satisfies basic human needs, including the need for identity, security, recognition, and personal development.[12]

Conflicting Theories of Change

Research currently underway suggests that a big part of the coordination problem rests at the conceptual level. The Reflecting on Peace Practice Project found that agencies have trouble coordinating in the field or even agreeing on an analysis of the problem, often because they are guided by radically different theories or assumptions about what causes conflict and how conflict can be resolved.[13] The project's findings suggest that a first step in working to achieve better coordination may lie in getting people to first recognize the "theories of change" that guide their own work:

> While peace practitioners select methods, approaches, and tactics that are rooted in a range of "theories" of how peace is achieved, in many (perhaps most) cases these theories are not necessarily

> conscious. Rather, they are embedded in the skills and approaches that they have learned, the capacities and "technologies" of their organizations, attachments to favorite methodologies, and the perspectives they bring to the peacebuilding process. They may also be dictated by international political dynamics and policies. A useful first step in enhancing the ability to develop effective strategies is to become more explicit about underlying assumptions about how change comes about – that is, theories of how to achieve peace. Such theories can take the simple format: We believe that by doing X (action) successfully, we will produce Y (movement towards peace).[14]

Often coordination is seen as a purely technical issue of engineering, that is, how to achieve the best information sharing structure. Or it is seen as a political problem, in terms of getting some groups to cede power and agree to be coordinated by others. What the "theories of change" concept points to instead is that people operate with different mental maps of what causes conflict, and therefore how to address it and what passes for coordination is often a dialogue of the deaf.

Organizational Factors

More mundane pathologies common to all organizations are also responsible for the lack of coherence in the efforts of the international community in a given peace mission, or within the various departments of the same organization.

Structural Barriers

Rigid organizational structures – including the stovepiping of departments and units, physical distance between organizations headquartered in different cities and field operations, the differing mandates of bureaus or divisions even within the same organization, and bureaucratic and daily operational constraints – tend to stifle innovation and favour the status quo. The considerable gap between policy formulators and implementers and between headquarters and field operations continues to undermine effectiveness. Among the problems identified by researchers are these:

- extremely weak knowledge management within organizations
- inadequate mechanisms to incorporate lessons learned
- little institutional memory about new programs implemented in various countries
- lack of a consistent and rigorous planning methodology and management capacity

- little country- or field-level interaction between program implementers, national authorities, and donors resulting in a multitude of unconnected programs and projects in various sectors
- lack of transparency and accountability.[15]

Organizational Cultures

There is a general tendency among organizations and even across units within the same organization to adopt substantially different planning and implementation terminology or to describe different processes and outcomes even when employing the same terminology. Examples abound. Civil-military coordination is relatively simple to conceptualize as an effort by civilian and military organizations to harmonize their operations, and yet de Coning has described it as a contested concept with many different, competing definitions and doctrines describing essentially the same activity.

Civil-Military Co-operation (CIMIC) is the terminology employed by NATO, most of the European Union (EU), and Canada. The United States (US) prefers Civil Military Operations (CMO), while the UN humanitarian community describes such activity as Humanitarian Civil-Military Coordination (CMCoord). The UN uses the acronym CIMIC when referring to "Civil-Military Coordination," whereas NATO uses CIMIC to describe "Civil-Military Co-operation." Here there are conceptual differences that matter growing out of fundamental differences in each organization's expectation and approach to the civil-military interface as it pertains to peacebuilding.[16]

Military culture and civilian cultures do not generally mesh seamlessly in conflict settings. There are inherent stressors between them owing to differences in mandates, objectives, methods of operation, and vocabulary. Operationally, aid agencies tend to be flexible, whereas the military functions in a top-down manner; the durations of stay of aid agencies can be for many years, while the military, on the other hand, prefers well defined end states and exit strategies; aid agencies have a culture of independence, while the military is hierarchical; and soldiers are armed when dealing with local actors, while aid and development workers are not.[17] Private contractors fall somewhere in between, depending on the nature of their assignment.

Organizational Independence

Some organizations consider their independence a higher priority than coordination with other organizations. They are not prepared to follow the lead of another organization. There is too a fear among NGOs of cooption and marginalization in some crisis regions where military forces have an overwhelming presence.

> This first became apparent in Afghanistan. NGOs previously open to dialogue with the military found their arguments for the importance of their independence and neutrality had limited impact, as US forces took on new small scale relief endeavours, and administration officials spoke of humanitarian NGOs as "force multipliers."[18]

The UN and international financial institutions (IFIs), especially the World Bank, have also come to play dominant roles in peacemaking vis-à-vis NGOs, especially where the strategic interests of powerful states are high. The transitional authority missions in Kosovo and East Timor enjoyed full control of virtually all aspects of state-building. The UN "performed functions related to civil administration, economic reconstruction, financial management, internal security, external security, international relations and treaty making, mounting of elections, administration of justice (including police and courts), and drafting of laws and constitutions." [19]

Some agencies argue that coordination (or integration, as in the UN system) is, by definition, a threat to humanitarian action because it undermines impartiality and represents a fundamental threat to the operational flexibility and physical safety of aid workers. In Afghanistan and Iraq in particular, but also to some extent in Liberia where the military mission is not considered impartial, the blocking and deliberate targeting of aid workers has resulted in unprecedented numbers of fatalities. The counter-argument posits that humanitarian space can be better protected through integrated structures as opposed to a fragmented approach and that the humanitarian perspective will have a more effective voice when at the same table with other elements of an integrated mission. There are also questions about the capability of humanitarian and aid organizations to provide for their own security in highly dangerous settings, the ethics of leaving some areas without assistance because they are too dangerous for aid workers, and the ability of soldiers to provide quality aid.

Competition for Resources

Organizations compete for financial resources, status, power, recognition, and influence. As one study of development and humanitarian action concludes,

> The most direct course for the expanding humanitarian sphere may be found in the large flows of donor aid to high profile emergencies, and the desire of UN development agencies to tap into these resources and establish themselves as players early on in the crisis. In the competitive environment that exists within the UN system of agencies and the larger aid community, to do otherwise is to risk marginalization.[20]

Competition also pits NGOs against generally higher paying organizations flying the banner of the UN, of donor government agencies, and increasingly, of private contracting firms. NGOs complain of losing in-country staff in particular to these competitors and of being lumped together with for-profit entities, as in Afghanistan where, until an NGO law was passed in 2005, they were officially categorized as belonging to the private sector. In fact, NGOs in Afghanistan pointed to an Afghan government study reporting that of the $3.9 billion of donor funding physically disbursed in the country by mid–2005, 45.5 per cent had gone directly to the UN, 30 per cent to the government, 16 per cent to private contractors, and only 9 per cent directly to NGOs.[21]

Inexperience and Lack of Proven Models

Organizations do not necessarily share a common understanding of the requirements or objectives of coordination. This problem is compounded by the fact that many organizations do not have established and well-defined working relationships with one another. Difficulties also arise when organizations are stretched beyond their traditional areas of expertise, as when development agencies take on security sector reform and the military becomes involved in state-building operations. Few models are available on best practice in combining and sequencing assistance, development, state-building, security, and stability in the so-called "failed state."

At levels below that of senior management in UN missions, there is less than full appreciation of the exact nature or function of UN integrated missions. NGOs and civil society organizations consulted by one study team were even more in the dark as to the exact form and function of integrated missions. Mission structures were found to be improvised. "In three different missions, senior management explained that it has applied best practices from other missions. Yet there was no evidence that such practices had ever been rigorously and systematically identified." Rather, the study team reveals, with reference to Liberia and Sudan, as well as to Cote d'Ivoire and Sierra Leone, where the problem was less pronounced, that "design reflects the inclinations and predilections of senior management, with little if any substantive reference to best practices, concepts of integration, or modern management practices." [22]

Idiosyncratic/Personality Factors

Success in cross-sectoral collaboration, particularly in the realm of civil-military relations, often depends on the personalities of the field level personnel and the liaison structures that are established. Reliance on individuals is a risky business, however, particularly among relief and development NGOs and other peacemaking organizations, given high rates of turnover, particularly among field staff.

Unco-operative attitudes are not uncommon within and across organizations. This may result from competition for resources, for power, and for notoriety, but it may also arise from personal likes and dislikes or stereotyping:

> Aid workers may consider the military arrogant or dominant and they may blame soldiers for a lack of true commitment and argue they should establish closer contact with the people rather than staying in the camp ... The military, on the other hand, may blame aid workers for being an uncoordinated, self-interested group of arrogant money-spenders that drive around in expensive cars and send impressive pictures to their constituencies without actually accomplishing much.[23]

Whatever the actual facts may be, collaboration is obviously more difficult to achieve where such views are held.

Findings on Coordination Problems in Afghanistan and Liberia

A research process culminating in a two-day practitioner workshop, "Coordinated Approaches to Security, Development, and Peacemaking: Lessons Learned from Afghanistan and Liberia," surveyed the practical dynamics of interagency and civil-military coordination in these two peace operations.[24] Thirty-five representatives of key civilian and military assistance actors involved in Liberia or Afghanistan together with experts on peacebuilding examined whether current coordination efforts amongst diverse assistance actors effectively support the interlinked goals of supporting security, development, and sustainable peace.

Any workshop represents a mere snapshot of a fast-moving and complex issue. The findings presented here represent a preliminary look at this complex problem and lay down some markers that we plan to build on through an ongoing learning effort. Two publications from the workshop review the experience to date and how the integrity and effectiveness of field coordination efforts among diverse assistance actors can be improved.[25] Some of the key findings related to civil-military coordination in particular from these findings are summarized below. However, two important caveats to the findings presented here must be stated upfront.

1. The focus of attention in the two cases was somewhat different. In Afghanistan, issues of civil-military coordination were a major focus, while in Liberia, issues of humanitarian coordination were more prominent. Nonetheless, an overall picture of the challenges and dilemmas of coordination in such settings was achieved.
2. The findings relate to field-level dynamics where programs are implemented–how headquarters policies actually play out in the field, rather than coordination efforts among agencies

in donor country capitals or within the global headquarters of international organizations in New York, Geneva, or Brussels.

Brief Overview of Lessons from Afghanistan

In Afghanistan, military, humanitarian, and development actors work side by side (though not necessarily together) in an environment with active insurgency in some regions and relative stability in others. In many policy areas, the agendas of violence reduction and the longer-term objectives of democratization, civil society building, and good governance clash as broad strategies are translated into concrete programs. Currently, dealing with widespread perceptions of corruption and improving governance is seen as the key to stability, alongside security and development gains. Tensions are high between military and some development actors over a perceived *militarization of aid* and the merging of military and assistance agendas in the Provincial Reconstruction Team (PRT) model, which is seen as the key mechanism for security and reconstruction outside of Kabul, but which critics claim has not produced the hoped-for gains in either security or reconstruction.

Examples of effective coordination cited were the health sector and the government's National Solidarity Program, where participatory, inclusive processes involving the government, donors, and implementing NGOs has resulted in significant "buy-in" from all key stakeholders. The record of coordination in many security-related areas is poor, however, as evidenced by a lack of coordination on counter-narcotics and diverse national strategies for the PRTs. These areas involve civilian and military actors with little history of positive co-operation, little common strategic vision, and a lack of effective inclusive and participatory planning processes.

Assessments strongly differed over capacity-building efforts and the PRTs, which are alternately seen by supporters as building blocs for an effective state, or by critics as superficial and externally driven approaches. Furthermore, there were strong disagreements over appropriate *means* to conduct programs, and *few common principles* guiding the efforts of military and development actors. More fundamentally, current coordination processes ignore differences in power and influence, undermining prospects for sincere communication, which is seen by many as requiring some level of horizontal relationship and transparency.

In the field, the perception is that the perspectives of military forces dominate and dramatically affect the work of aid organizations. NATO perceives "little real interest" in coordination from other actors and finds itself in the position of reluctantly leading the overall strategy "by default" and being resented for "taking control." By virtue of its enormous resources and dominant military presence, US policy often leads but has avoided an explicit leadership role in the broader nation-building efforts.

Given these dynamics, there is little trust amongst actors that coordination efforts on offer are not simply an attempt by powerful political actors to exert control over the activities of smaller players.

Brief Overview of Lessons from Liberia

In Liberia, violence has been quelled in the aftermath of the 2003 Comprehensive Peace Agreement and the presence of 15,000 UN peacekeeping forces under the UN Mission in Liberia (UNMIL) mission. Basic security has been consolidated, but long-term stability rests on meeting daunting humanitarian and development needs and on building legitimate and effective government institutions, especially the army, police, and justice system. Currently, UNMIL's large force is key to providing security with domestic institutions still very weak and relief and development efforts heavily dependent on the UN and NGOs. Examples of effective coordination are to be found in humanitarian sectors, notably health and education, where there is a history of engagement and where dedicated UN-led humanitarian coordination mechanisms provide a forum for common analysis and strategy-making amongst civilian assistance actors.

Security sector activities are reportedly plagued by poor coordination, however, with inclusive consultative processes largely lacking, undermining public trust in army and police reform, for example. Problems identified include: a lack of a common strategic vision between the government, the UN, and external NGOs; the limitations of existing coordination mechanisms in going beyond information sharing and dealing with power asymmetries between UN agencies, government, and NGOs to create a truly joint vision; fundamental differences in how problems and solutions are defined between key actors; and a tendency for external actors to dominate in defining frameworks and strategies, promoting a "false coherence" that is counterproductive.[26]

There is also in Liberia a fundamental difference between actors on appropriate roles for external actors in sensitive political decisions as well as a perception that even though current humanitarian coordination processes have had some success, they often serve the UN mission's agenda over that of NGOs and local civil society. The preponderant US role in all areas of assistance to Liberia continues to be a key factor, and coordination between US initiatives and the UN mission is seen as problematic at times. Finally, the mismatch of international assistance with actual needs has been underscored by various commentators, with observations that today Liberia needs more engineers and development specialists than it does military peacekeepers.

Coordination Processes and Outcomes

The diverse assistance actors that make up international peace missions each have unique mandates, accountability to different constituencies, and are motivated by different models of how to promote change. These fundamental incompatibilities between international military forces, political and diplomatic actors, and relief and development agencies make effective communication difficult, and significantly block the realization of coordination and collaboration in the field.

At the broadest level, the workshop revealed a substantial gap between policies institutionalizing coordination and coherence amongst the headquarters (HQ) of assistance actors and the messy reality of very little effective coordination between civilian and military actors in the field. This result echoes the findings of an in-depth report subsequently published by the International Peace Academy (IPA) in July 2007 that examined in detail the evolution of current "whole-of-government approaches" in seven major donor countries, including Canada and the US, and found that across the board, the rhetoric of coherence within departments of donor governments far outstrips the reality.[27]

Clearly, mission-wide coordination is far more complex than these efforts towards coherence within individual donor governments, and the gaps in existing knowledge are immense. Mission-wide coordination involves multiple bilateral efforts by major donors like the United States and smaller ones like the United Kingdom (UK), Canada, Germany, etc.; multi-lateral agencies like the UN, the EU, and the World Bank; security organizations such as NATO; and a huge array of international NGOs, usually working with local organizations, not to mention the central and subnational governments of the host country. The challenges of understanding the complex dynamics of these processes are considerable, but doing so is critical to improving the impact of international efforts for sustainable peace.

In brief, the examination of the Afghanistan and Liberia cases showed that existing field coordination processes in the main have two outcomes:

- They result in mere "information sharing" and have no real coordination impact; and/or
- They produce a kind of forced, "false coherence," referring to superficial changes in language and formal adherence to new frameworks, both driven by the agenda of the actor with the most power and resources.

Blocks to Coordination in Afghanistan and Liberia

Some of the blocks to effective coordination identified in the two cases examined derive from the factors noted earlier on – different organizational cultures, styles, and approaches, as well as structural issues such as the nature of the overall objectives being pursued and the tools utilized. Very different time frames and criteria for success are two more key areas where these incompatibilities manifest themselves in very concrete ways and may be insurmountable.

For international military forces, time frames are generally short, with military rotations commonly of six months' durations and commanders pressured to show results in that period. Furthermore, for the military, primary objectives are to protect the national security of their home government and populations, and criteria for success ultimately has to focus on those points of reference. For relief and development actors, time frames are generally longer term – while emergency relief aims to save lives immediately and are expected to show immediate results, development initiatives commonly are assessed over periods of three, five, or even ten years. Finally, for relief and development agencies generally, the primary focus of concern is ostensibly the welfare of populations in the recipient country, whereas the interests of the donor country or organization may be more pronounced among defence and security actors.

Tellingly, most examples of poor coordination noted in the two cases involved areas relating to security sector reform where agencies had little history of contact and where models for coordination and participatory public processes are very new and untested. In these areas, there is a lack of "holistic" engagement between security-related and development-related agencies such that mutually agreeable and reinforcing approaches cannot be ironed out.

The review of experience in these two countries led to the identification of the following as the fundamental barriers to coordination.

1. Lack of Common Purpose: Assistance actors do not agree on the purpose of coordination efforts in the first place. Some emphasize minimalist goals of simple information exchange and mutual awareness, while others' aims extend to joint analysis of problems, joint strategy making and prioritization of tasks, a clear division of labour, and sequencing of interventions. Without transparency and trust about the purpose, well-intentioned coordination efforts often paradoxically result in "false coherence," or the superficial commitment to common strategies on paper only.

With respect to civil-military coordination in the field, common aims were largely absent. Military actors expressed frustration with coordination exercises for amounting to "just information sharing," while many NGOs saw the purpose of such efforts as rightly limited to information sharing and expressed more concern about the quality and reliability of the information. It is striking that for the military, these meetings are aimed at enhancing impacts, deciding a functional division of labour, and realizing synergies in the work, while for the development NGOs, they are about mutual understanding and awareness, building reliable lines of communication, and sometimes "minimizing the harm from the military's involvement in relief work." [28] For strictly humanitarian relief NGOs, their goals in such interactions are to exchange a minimal amount of information so that the NGOs and aid beneficiaries "do not get shot at" and so the "military understands our approach."

2. *Lack of a Level Playing Field in Consultative Processes*: Actors had very different sensitivities to the power asymmetries inherent in coordination efforts. NGOs and host government representatives emphasized power differentials, while international political and military actors treated coordination largely as a technical exercise that was power-neutral. Not dealing directly with the power differential may be counterproductive – as the "elephant in the room," it is likely to undermine trust.

3. *Different Guiding Principles:* Civilian and military assistance actors operate on the basis of fundamentally different principles for decision making. The principles of "neutrality" and "humanitarian need" that humanitarian and relief groups use to allocate aid clashes at times with the principle of "UN endorsed partiality" guiding the state-building activities of diplomatic, political, and military actors in their support for the government. Furthermore, the widely accepted principle of local ownership is difficult in practice, given the weak state of government institutions and the fact that the expressed priorities of national and provincial governments and grassroots communities often conflict, with international agencies in effect responding to different "local voices." While most agencies fall back on a pragmatic "greater good" orientation, there may be little agreement amongst assistance actors on just what the greater good is, given their different values, orientations, constituencies, mandates, and time frames. There are also serious concerns about who will be held accountable for making ethical choices about sensitive political issues, given that only national governments are held accountable by their publics, not international agencies or militaries.

Factors Supporting Coordination

Diverse civilian and military assistance actors pointed to the following attributes of "effective coordination" they had experienced in the field. When synthesized, this provided almost a checklist that could be used to build on the strengths and identify the weaknesses of existing coordination efforts.

According to workshop participants from both military and civilian agencies, effective coordination involves the following:

- informality and "face to face" time
- getting "straight information" from someone you trust, not agency "propaganda"

- transparency and horizontal relationships amongst agencies/ people
- time – learning how to coordinate takes time and is a learning process
- inclusiveness – all key stakeholders being involved early in the process
- sincere motives to improve program impacts (vs. funding, competition, credit, egos)
- good negotiation skills, ability to articulate arguments and win over others
- common knowledge of the issues amongst participants
- an ability to accept criticism from others
- internal consensus on key issues existing within agencies and networks
- higher decision makers allowing for flexibility and negotiation at the field level
- continuity of service and less turnover of field personnel.

KEY PRACTICAL AND CONCEPTUAL CHALLENGES

Our findings to date point to four key challenges in better understanding the real prospects for cross-agency and civil-military coordination in international missions for peace.

1. The Mixed Consequences Challenge

Efforts to promote more coordination and integration of multiple assistance actors working in war-to-peace transitions seem on the surface to be an uncontroversial agenda. In reality, they present real tradeoffs and can have negative consequences for other equally important agendas. As the cases noted here show, the humanitarian dilemma over compromising humanitarian impartiality, the human rights dilemma over working with war leaders, and the local ownership dilemma over letting local perspectives and "ways of doing things" lead, identified in general by other reports, are abundantly present in Liberia and Afghanistan.[29] They emerge in the many examples of programs where there were fundamental differences in strategies and the weighting of means and ends between the key assistance communities. Some examples raised of where the different goals and ethics of assistance actors clashed were:

- working with government-allied warlords to quickly build a road considered to be key to development prospects
- pushing IDP repatriation to meet a political timetable for elections rather than in response to humanitarian needs
- "bribing" war leaders with seats in Parliament so they will lay down arms
- transforming wartime militias into national police and army units
- recruiting skilled people who over-represent certain ethnic groups into these new security institutions
- "rewarding" ex-combatants with employment in development projects to reduce threats to stability, and
- ignoring or accepting corrupt practices because they are more efficient, or are the "way of doing things here."

2. *The Policy Practice Challenge*

The gap between policies institutionalizing coordination and coherence amongst the headquarters of assistance actors and actual practice in the field is real. In both cases, national governments and international actors have agreed formal frameworks for the statebuilding/peacebuilding effort that show how political reforms, economic development, security, governance, and national reconciliation are critical "pillars" of national recovery. These frameworks are helpful in establishing the highest-level goals, but they do not represent multi-actor agreement on strategies – because there are differences in terms of the weight of different pillars or sectors, and especially over how to actually accomplish these goals. Consequently, these commonly agreed frameworks for the recovery effort do not automatically translate into common goals between actors engaged in different sectors and pillars.

As the two cases show, coordination processes often assume agreement among actors on strategies and do not provide opportunities for inclusive and meaningful multi-stakeholder dialogue on these more fundamental issues. Additionally, power asymmetries block real dialogue and limit the ability of existing coordination processes to achieve some level of common intent. Cross-agency dialogue that might help arrive at consensus on strategies is hard and requires dedicated skills, procedures, and incentives. The review of experience here suggests there are few dedicated efforts at the field level to promote such inclusive approaches to dialogue and consensus building among field actors.

As well, the field-headquarters relationship too often reflects a top-down flow of policy directives that often translate into changes in language and formal adherence to new frameworks without having achieved "buy in" from field personnel to the intent of policy makers. The experience shows a need to shift the relationship between field and headquarters within many agencies to promote a two-way information flow with the goal being to bring field perspectives more into the HQ level debates and vice versa. The goal would be to help decision makers at both levels better understand important factors that must shape policy responses. In a rapidly changing environment, the importance of field personnel to be able to understand and interpret the intent of a policy is key to flexible and effective responses. The inflexibility of policies set at headquarters level was cited as sometimes rendering dialogue over strategies amongst field actors "pointless."

3. The Evaluation Challenge

Effective coordination between security and development actors presumably means more effective work than is possible without coordination. This requires evaluating the impacts of projects involving significant coordination efforts on the broader peace. However, as noted, this is an area where there are few credible methodologies, and there is generally substantial pessimism that such impacts are possible to trace at the level of individual projects. Among assistance actors in Liberia and Afghanistan as well, coordination is assumed to be a good thing, but equally clear was that different actors used dramatically different criteria for what effective coordination looks like. As well, most of these criteria focus on coordination processes rather than outcomes.

The findings here show the importance of continued effort in assessing the positive benefits of coordination on peace, and equally important, the negative impacts that may inadvertently arise – on beneficiaries directly, in terms of undermining key project goals, or on prospects for peace more broadly. This is critical because, without evidence that striving to attain linkage between diverse assistance efforts matters to their "bottom line," few actors will want to invest the considerable energy and political will involved, or be willing to accept tradeoffs and even negative consequences for other important goals. Methodologies for evaluating coordination success and failure remain a very big knowledge gap that needs to be addressed. Finally, evaluation efforts should not be seen as an "add-on" or as a donor-driven agenda, but rather, as critical to helping coordination efforts find their way. Rigorous efforts to clearly define what goals coordinated projects are fostering and how we can tell if these are achieved will help all involved better define what is desired and reduce the ambiguity and "faith-based" approach surrounding existing coordination efforts.

4. The Challenge of the Role of NGOs

Today, NGOs are critical actors in war-to-peace transitions in that they represent a large proportion of the implementation and service delivery capacity of the international assistance enterprise from the earliest emergency stage to the handoff to host government institutions. For example, a recent World Bank report noted that in Afghanistan, money flowing to NGOs accounted for 27 per cent of development aid in 2005, but the magnitude of the NGO role in Afghanistan only becomes clear when looking at specific sectors; for example, in health care some estimates suggest that 90 per cent of total health service delivery is carried out by NGOs, and in other sectors and major programmes, as much as 75–80 per cent of the funds are contracted through NGOs.[30] Though, as often noted, they represent a fantastically diverse number and array of organizations and agendas, recent years have seen the growth of NGO networks united by common principles and practices both internationally and in-country – as with the NGO coordination bodies currently operating in Afghanistan and Liberia. Though often engaged in multi-agency coordination processes with governmental and intergovernmental actors, NGOs still do not have a lot of power at the formal tables where strategies are decided, though they have significant power in shaping how these strategies turn out in the field.

Spheres for Improvement in Coordination Processes

The experience reviewed in the workshop suggests some key areas for coordination where new approaches seem necessary. These relate to people, processes, structures, and principles.

People

The skills and approaches used and the personalities of the people involved matter to coordination outcomes. Participants mentioned individuals (whether military or humanitarian personnel or diplomats) who, with their energy, initiative, and communication skills, had been very effective at coordination in the field. In fact, good people can often overcome bad systems. But across the two cases generally, the level of skills that groups have to bridge the big divide between unlike actors renders coordination highly problematic. Recruitment should emphasize consensus-building abilities and interpersonal and communication skills if agency personnel are to bridge major organizational divides and foster coordination. The cultivation of "good people" in these roles can also be supported through dedicated training in the necessary skills (negotiation, conflict management, consensus-building) and through rigorous screening to be sure the right people are situated in the right positions. It is imperative that properly vetted and trained personnel who can exercise the kind of leadership that cross-organizational and cross-cultural collaboration requires be placed in leadership positions at all levels.

There is not enough focus on the skills required for managing conflict and engaging in consensus-building processes in the way that coordination efforts are currently conceived. This is the case with civil-military coordination, but also among UN agencies and NGOs engaged in coordination exercises within their own community and with other actors. The prevalence of "badly run meetings" in field coordination efforts across the board was noted in the workshop, as was a general inability to "win others over with arguments" and to "accept criticism." These necessary skills should be cultivated among senior as well as junior personnel so they have the ability to engage effectively in efforts to communicate and coordinate with diverse agencies in the field. An additional consideration is that international agencies are staffed with people from a very wide range of cultural backgrounds and perspectives on power, authority, and coordination, and these differences need to be dealt with in trying to support a more inclusive, consensus-seeking process of interagency dialogue on if and how to collaborate.

Processes

The processes used for interaction are a critical part of effective coordination. Experience from both Liberia and Afghanistan shows that assistance actors from all perspectives are currently ill-served by existing top-down approaches to coordination, often resulting in a "false coherence," a superficial commitment to common strategies on paper only. At best, most current approaches in Afghanistan achieve information sharing between agencies, but they do not yield the kind of basic agreement on strategies and the "buy in" necessary for a coherent response. In Liberia, humanitarian coordination is an instructive example in that outcomes are somewhat better due to inclusive planning processes, for example, the Consolidated Appeals Process (CAP) and the Common Humanitarian Action Plan (CHAP) led by the Humanitarian Coordination Section within UNMIL in Liberia, but developed by the dedicated United Nations Office for the Coordination of Humanitarian Affairs (UNOCHA). The CAP and CHAP processes require UN agencies and NGOs to jointly define the situation and agree on priority needs, a very important process of creating some minimal common understanding of the problems and the solutions needed. That experience, reviewed in the Liberia case study, nevertheless illustrates that even between like actors (UN and NGO humanitarian agencies), questions of power asymmetry can undermine the integrity of coordination processes and cause some actors to withdraw; but overall the process of dialogue fostered by these mechanisms produces a humanitarian strategy with some basic level of buy in from NGOs, the UN, and donors. These processes require intense efforts and dedicated personnel and resources, however, and are time consuming even among the UN humanitarian agencies, OCHA, and humanitarian and development NGOs that exhibit sufficiently like backgrounds, principles, and modes of operation.

In Afghanistan, what stops the key political and military actors and a representative group of NGOs from sitting down to do a similar common assessment of problems and needs? From the experience reviewed, the sense is that the political and military actors sit down and create the strategy, likely acknowledging advocacy from civil society and NGOs that they have invited at various points, but without direct representation in a way commensurate with their importance in the whole implementation enterprise. Consultations are too often held with the development community, in particular the NGOs, only after the fact and are narrowly focused on implementation. A case in point is the proposed Afghan Development Zones model, where NATO's ISAF aimed to facilitate development efforts by devising a plan it thought met the needs and interests of other actors, only to face strong resistance from development actors. Effective, consensus-based planning processes in other fields show that this approach rarely works, and transparency and horizontal relationships are often critical to effective coordination. Not bringing the aid implementers into the up-front planning and not offering them a role as strategies are developed makes getting a buy-in from this critical group a difficult proposition. They are much more likely to resist strategies decided elsewhere.

Another important dynamic related to coordination processes in Afghanistan and Liberia was that different assistance communities generally had different assumptions about the very goals of the effort. The fact that groups often do not even share the same assumptions significantly reduces the chances of useful coordination emerging from such interactions.

Some analysts have argued that in cases where agencies are not committed to a common goal, explicit coordination is not appropriate or useful.[31] However, because the effects of the work of agencies in the security-development interface are so closely linked, they cannot realistically separate themselves. If they choose not to interact at some minimal level, they still suffer the consequences of poor coordination. What is needed is a way to work side by side that advances their mutually supportive agendas but one that is different from the integration agenda/top-down command currently being pushed in some quarters or the overly optimistic model of self-coordination driven by awareness of the benefits among various actors. What is needed is a process that recognizes the inherent linkage between security and development efforts and strives to maximize the positive benefits from this and minimize the negative.

Also critical are sincere, even-handed, and widely inclusive consultative processes for devising strategies in a given area and some incentive for all groups to engage in these.

It is imperative that in trying to make progress on the coordination issue in international peace operations, we do not overestimate the importance of coordination amongst external actors. We need to keep in mind the provocative research finding that in recent international peace missions, the strength of internal processes was more important for successful recovery than coordination amongst external actors.[32] Some participants in the workshop pointed out that in both Afghanistan and Liberia, there has been little effort to foster this kind of internal debate inclusive of government, opposition, and civil society perspectives over how to create the new state and its institutions such that the internal actors can reach some basic common positions on what they need from international actors, and what they do not.

Structures

The structures defining civil-military interaction are also a critical element. The Afghan and Liberian experience reviewed shows the utility of a common organizational structure in affecting the complex interface between security, development, and peacemaking. The UN-integrated mission structures in Liberia provide a way to deal with the big differences among diverse actors in a common organizational structure, though we learned little of the dynamics and negotiation between the civilian and military arms of the mission. The Afghanistan case, by contrast, shows the immense difficulties of direct interface between civilian and military actors as occurs in the PRTs, and also of working on peacebuilding issues as a loose coalition of diverse states with separate policies.

One important structural issue particularly directed at the military is the need to more clearly separate out security and development roles in practice, though they are tied conceptually. The military should focus its efforts on establishing security and resist the temptation or the push from political masters to sell its mission in humanitarian or development terms. Many recent studies have shown that populations in conflict zones appreciate security assistance first and foremost for its own sake.[33] The selling of the Afghan mission as a humanitarian effort to domestic constituencies in NATO member states is very problematic for humanitarian and development agencies, as noted throughout this report. Discussions revealed, however, that it is also not fully supported by many military personnel, as it forces them to take on roles they are ill-equipped for and that create major problems with the other key actors whose role in relief and development is critical to the success of the overall outcome.

Another structural issue relates to the financial mechanisms available to both security- and development-focused actors. One structural reason noted why relief and development actors cannot deliver aid as quickly as the military claims it "needs" is that funding mechanisms for aid and development work often require much longer lead times, while military commanders often have access to substantial discretionary funds. Donors should consider making available more rapidly available standby funds, and both donors and NGOs should develop mechanisms that would allow NGOs to respond more quickly to urgent needs in areas where there is an international military presence and preclude the need or temptation for militaries to fill these roles themselves.

Principles

The lack of common principles to guide decision-making amongst diverse actors is another key problem area suggested by the experience reviewed. With some actors basing the daily strategic and operational decisions that arise on the principle of "the will of the international community as expressed by UN resolutions" and others on "humanitarian independence and neutrality" and still others on a more flexible, subjective "greater good" orientation, some clarity on basic principles is needed so that, at a minimum, the efforts of various actors do not undermine each other.

As both cases noted, the interdependence of security and development forces disparate assistance actors to attempt to coordinate, even though they often do not share common objectives. One clear difference amongst agencies that blocks coordination is the relative weight different agencies place on means and ends. Agencies that place great importance on a specific means of implementing aid work are not willing to synchronize their efforts with other actors that do not share these values. Other actors are more willing to compromise on the means in order to get things done and get results. The example discussed during the workshop of building a strategic road in Afghanistan to open up a critical area of the country to development cast these differences in stark relief, with some groups emphasizing the actual road as the only important end, while other groups emphasized that the way the road was built was equally important in terms of whether it reinforced the power of warlords and corrupt practices or worsened ethnic divisions. If agencies could define some "accepted means" to conduct programs and lay out some clear, basic, common principles, this could assist groups in working "side by side" without undermining each other, even in the absence of common goals. Such an approach has been suggested by Rob Ricigliano, employing his concept of "networks of effective action," for peacebuilding actors united by some basic principles, but to date no test case has been undertaken.[34]

Yet finding common principles between such diverse actors is still a difficult enterprise. A general commitment to "building peace" or "helping the people" in Afghanistan or Liberia is not enough and there must be some agreement on means as well.

In terms of principles, a key challenge for the humanitarian and development community is to clarify for themselves and other actors how the concepts of neutrality and humanitarian space apply to development and reconstruction activities in such ambiguous, half-war/half-peace settings. Development is an expressly political activity, working with the recognized government on building an effective state infrastructure, services, and a functioning economy. Currently, agencies engaged in development work still defend the importance of neutrality and strict separation from the military, but while the need for neutrality and independence of purely humanitarian actors is largely accepted, this position for development actors is greeted with skepticism. There is confusion among development agencies themselves, it seems, as to the principles that should guide this development role.

Reconstruction, the primary mandate of the military in aid, is a final major grey area since often only the military have the capacity to undertake certain large-scale reconstruction efforts quickly. There are many questions that the aid community does not seem to have clear answers to. Do reconstruction activities require neutrality, and if so, why? What can be done, when? Is there a legitimate role for the military in the provision of aid when there are no humanitarian actors in a setting to provide relief? Is humanitarian space really possible in these environments? The aid community, as part of an improved interagency dialogue, needs to develop more clarity internally on these questions.

Equally, international military forces should clarify the principles that guide their involvement in these contexts. What principles should guide the military's non-military operations to ensure they contribute positively to the broader stabilization effort? How does the interdependence of security and development in these settings change the way such operations need to be planned and decisions made?

CONCLUSION

The insights presented here illustrate how current efforts to improve coordination and integration amongst international and national agencies in practice neglect key process issues and best practices. As well, they often replicate power relations that block real dialogue amongst and between both architects and implementers of peacebuilding efforts. Little progress on effective coordination can be achieved until important differences between mandates, roles, and values held by diverse civilian and military international assistance actors are voiced and a sincere dialogue over both opportunities and limits to coordinated efforts can take place. Organizational stovepipes, power politics, and the current mechanistic structures and processes for coordination make this type of sincere dialogue difficult, but these obstacles must be overcome if international efforts are to provide truly effective support of sustainable peace to conflict-affected countries.

NOTES

Much of the material in this article comes from Olson and Gregorian, *Side by Side or Together? Working for Security, Development and Peace in Liberia and Afghanistan*, available from <http://www.ucalgary.ca/pdsp/files/pdsp/sidebysideortogether_jan2008.pdf>.

1. Centre on International Cooperation, *Annual Review of Global Peace Operations*, 6, 2006.
2. Michael Lund, *What Kind of Peace is Being Built? Assessing the Record of Post-Conflict Peacebuilding, Charting Future Directions* (Ottawa: International Development Research Centre, Jan. 2003).
3. This term is used in different ways by different researchers, governments, and practitioners. For some, it refers to the overall engagement of the international community in a given country to consolidate peace; that is elections, economic liberalization, security reform, governance, development, human rights assistance, etc. For others, peacebuilding is a particular kind of programming engaging people in a range of activities that have the explicit aim of fostering peaceful relations.
4. Telephone interview with a representative of a major international NGO with programs across Afghanistan who asked to remain anonymous.
5. Stewart Patrick and Kaysie Brown, *Greater than the Sum of Its Parts? Assessing "Whole of Government" Approaches to Fragile States*, 18 (New York: International Peace Academy, 2007).
6. Bruce D. Jones, "The Changing Role of the UN in Protracted Crises," *HPG Research Briefing*, no. 17, July 2004.
7. Necla Tschirgi, *Security and Development Policies: Untangling the Relationship*, 5 (New York: International Peace Academy [IPA], 2005).
8. Ibid., 12–13.
9. Roland Paris, "*Understanding The 'Coordination Problem' in Post War State-Building*," Research Partnership on Postwar State-building (RPPS), 10, <http://state-building.org>.
10. Abby Stoddard and Adele Harmer, *Room to Manoeuvre: Challenges of Linking Humanitarian Action and Post-Conflict Recovery in the New Global Security Environment*, 10, United Nations Development Programme, Human Development Report Office, Occasional paper, 2005.

11. Cedric de Coning, "Civil-Military Coordination and UN Peacebuilding Operations," *Durban Accord*, <http://jha.ac/articles/a183.pdf>.
12. See John Burton, *Conflict: Basic Human Needs* (New York: St. Martin's Press, 1990).
13. Mary Anderson and Lara Olson, *Confronting War: Critical Lessons for Peace Practitioners,* Collaborative for Development Action, 2003, <www.cdainc.com>.
14. Peter Woodrow, "Theories of Change/Theories of Peacebuilding," Reflecting on Peace Practice Project Paper, CDA Collaborative Learning Projects, 2006.
15. Tschirgi, *Untangling the Relationship*, 12–13.
16. Cedric de Coning, "Civil-Military Coordination," 6.
17. Georg Frerks, Bart Klem, Stefan van Laar, and Marleen van Klingeren, *Principles and Pragmatism Civil-Military Action in Afghanistan and Liberia*, 35. Study commissioned by Cordaid, May 2006, <www.cordaid.nl>.
18. Stoddard, *Room to Manoeuvre,* 13.
19. Bruce D. Jones, *The UN's Evolving Role in Peace and Security: Background Note,* <http://www.cic.nyu.edu/internationalsecurity/docs/The%20UN%20and%20International%20Security%20in%20the%201990s.doc>.
20. Stoddard, *Room to Manoeuvre,* 5.
21. Lara Olson, "Fighting For Humanitarian Space: NGOS in Afghanistan," *Journal of Military and Strategic Studies* 9, no. 1 (2006): 20.
22. Stoddard, *Room to Manoeuvre.*
23. Espen Barth Eide and others, *Report on Integrated Missions: Practical Perspectives and Recommendations*, 36, Independent Study for the Expanded UN ECHA Core Group, 2005, <http://www.reliefweb.int/rw/lib.nsf/db900SID/SODA-6CK7SK?OpenDocument>.
24. Mar. 30 and 31 at the University of Calgary's Centre for Military and Strategic Studies (CMSS), in conjunction with its Washington, D.C.-based partner, the Institute of World Affairs (IWA). Generous financial support for this workshop was provided by the Centre for Military and Strategic Studies, the Canadian International Development Agency's (CIDA) Conference Secretariat, the Department of National Defence's Security and Defence Forum, NATO's Public Diplomacy Division, and several departments of the University of Calgary: the Faculty of Social Sciences, the International Centre, and the Political Science Department. Equally generous in-kind support was extended by the Institute of World Affairs, and many participating agencies covered the time and costs of their personnel.
25. Policy Brief, Oct. 2007, "Beyond Information Sharing & False Coherence: Interagency Coordination in International Peace Missions," Workshop Report, Oct. 2007; *Side by Side or Together? Working for Security, Development and Peace in Liberia and Afghanistan,* <http://www.ucalgary.ca/pdsp/publications>.
26. This useful term was first suggested by a participant in the Mar. 2007 workshop–Cheyanne Church, Lecturer in Human Security, Fletcher School, Tufts University, Boston.

27. Patrick and Brown, *Greater than the Sum of Its Parts: Assessing "Whole of Government" Approaches to Fragile States* (New York: International Peace Academy, July 2007).
28. As observed by one workshop participant.
29. Eide, *Report on Integrated Missions*, 10.
30. World Bank, "Service Delivery and Governance at the Sub-National Level in Afghanistan," p. 29, July 2007.
31. Susan Allen Nan, "Intervention Coordination," Intractable Conflict Knowledge Base, 2003, <www.beyondintractability.org>; <http://crinfo.beyondintractability.org/essay/intervention_coordination> [June 2007].
32. Chetan Kumar, "What Really Works in Preventing and Rebuilding Failed States?" *Occasional Paper Series*, No. 2, p. 7, Washington: Woodrow Wilson International Centre for Scholars, Dec. 2006.
33. Antonio Domini, Larry Minear, Ian Smillie, Ted van Baarda, and Anthony C. Welch. *Mapping the Security Environment: Understanding the Perceptions of Local Communities, Peace Support Operations and Assistance Agencies*, (New York: Feinstein International Famine Centre, June 2005), <http://www.mod.uk/NR/rdonlyres/17F3955C-09AC-4405-B375-FD5A4FACAA8D/0/map_security_envirnmnt_june05.pdf> [Jan. 2007]; see also Diana Chigas, *Has Peacebuilding Made a Difference in Kosovo*? (Cambridge, MA: CDA Collaborative Learning Projects, July 2006), <http://www.cdainc.com/cdawww/pdf/book/cdapeacebuildingreportkosovo_Pdf4.pdf> [Feb. 2007].
34. Robert Ricigliano. "Networks of Effective Action: Implementing an Integrated Approach to Peacebuilding," *Security Dialogue*, No. 34, 2003.

Bibliography

This represents sources used for the overall research project on which this article is based, and though all sources below are not directly referenced in the article, they are included to serve as a resource on these issues.

All, Pamela R., Daniel T. Miltenberger, and Thomas G. Weiss. *IGOs, NGOs and the Military in Peace and Relief Operations*. Washington: United States Institute of Peace Press, 2000.

Active Learning Network for Accountability and Performance in Humanitarian Action (ALNAP). Key Lessons from Evaluations of Humanitarian Action in Liberia, Sept. 2003. <http://www.humanitarianinfo.org/Liberia/infocentre/general/docs/liberiasynthesis_final.pdf>.

Anderson, Mary B. *Do No Harm: How Aid Can Support Peace–Or War.* Boulder, CO: Lynne Rienner Publishing, 2002.

Anderson, Mary B. and Lara Olson. *Confronting War: Critical Lessons for Peace Practitioners.* Cambridge, MA: Collaborative for Development Action, 2002. <www.cdainc.com>.

Bellamy, Alex, Paul Williams, and Stuart Griffin. *Understanding Peacekeeping.* Cambridge, MA: Polity Press, 2002.

Burton, John. *Conflict: Basic Human Needs.* New York: St. Martin's Press, 1990.

Cahill, Kevin M. ed. *Traditions, Values, and Humanitarian Action.* New York: Fordham University Press, 2003.

Canadian Peacebuilding Coordinating Committee. *NGO/Government Dialogue on Provincial Reconstruction Teams (PRTs) in Afghanistan and the Militarization of Humanitarian Assistance: Final Report.* 4 Dec. 2003.

Centre on International Cooperation. *Annual Review of Global Peace Operations, 2006.* Boulder, CO: Lynne Rienner Publishers, 2006.

Chayes, Antonia Handler and Abram Chayes. *Planning for Intervention: International Cooperation in Conflict Management.* The Hague: Kluwer Law International, 1999.

Chesterman, Simon, Michel Ignatieff, and Ramesh Chandra, eds. *Making States Work: State Failure and the Crisis of Governance.* Tokyo: United Nations University Press, 2005.

Covey, Jock, Michael J. Dziedzic, and Leonard R. Hawley, eds. *The Quest for Viable Peace: International Intervention and Strategies for Conflict Transformation.* Washington, DC: United States Institute of Peace Press, 2005.

Chigas, Diana. *Has Peacebuilding Made a Difference in Kosovo?* Cambridge, MA: CDA Collaborative Learning Projects, July 2006. <http://www.cdainc.com/cdawww/pdf/book/cdapeacebuildingreportkosovo_Pdf4.pdf> [Feb. 2007].

Crocker, Chester A., Fen Osler Hampson, and Pamela R. Aall. *Grasping the Nettle: Analyzing Cases of Intractable Conflict.* Washington, DC: United States Institute of Peace Press, 2005.

de Coning, Cedric. Civil-Military Coordination and UN Peacebuilding Operations. In *International Peacekeeping: The Yearbook of International Peace Operations,* Volume 11, ed. H. Langholtz, B. Kondoch, and A. Wells, 47–69. Bruxelles: Koninklijke Brill N.V., 2007.

-----. Integrated Missions, Coherence, Coordination and Complex Peacebuilding Systems. Paper presented at the Public Administration Meets Peacebuilding: Peace Operations as Political and Managerial Challenges Conference, University of Konstanz, Germany, 15–16 June 2007.

-----. Civil-Military Coordination and UN Peacebuilding Operations. *African Journal on Conflict Resolution* 5, no. 2: Dec. 2005.

Domini, Antonio, Norah Niland, and Karin Wermester, eds. *Nation-Building Unraveled? Aid, Peace and Justice in Afghanistan.* Bloomfield, CT: Kumarian Press, 2004.

Domini, Antonio, Larry Minear, Ian Smillie, Ted van Baarda, and Anthony C. Welch. *Mapping the Security Environment: Understanding the Perceptions of Local Communities. Peace Support Operations and Assistance Agencies.* New York: Feinstein International Famine Centre, June 2005. <http://www.mod.uk/NR/rdonlyres/17F3955C-09AC-4405-B375-FD5A4FACAA8D/0/map_security_envirnmnt_june05.pdf>.

Doyle, Michael W. and Nicholas Sambanis. *Making War and Building Peace: United Nations Peace Operations.* Princeton, NJ: Princeton University Press, 2006.

Duffield, Mark. *Global Governance and the New Wars: The Merging of Development and Security.* New York: Zed Books, 2001.

Durch, William J. *UN Peacekeeping, American Policy and the Uncivil Wars of the 1990s.* New York: Palgrave Macmillan, 2006.

Dziedzic, Michael J. and Colonel Michael K. Siedel. *Provincial Reconstruction Teams and Military Relations with International and Non-Governmental Organizations in Afghanistan,* Special Report 147. New York: U.S. Institute of Peace, Sept. 2005. <http://www.usip.org/pubs/specialreports/sr147.html>.

Easterly, William. *The White Man's Burden: Why the West's Efforts to Aid the Rest Have Done So Much Ill and So Little Good.* New York: Penguin, 2007.

Eide, Espen Barth, Anja Therese Kapersen, Randolph Kent, and Karin von Hipple. *Report on Integrated Missions: Practical Perspectives and Recommendations.* UN Office for the Coordination of Humanitarian Affairs (OCHA) <http://www.reliefweb.int/rw/lib.nsf/db900SID/SODA-6CK7SK?OpenDocument>.

-----. *Report on Integrated Missions: Practical Perspectives and Recommendations.* Independent Study for the Expanded UN ECHA Core Group. Oslo: Norwegian Institute of International Affairs (NUPI), May 2005.

Frerks, Georg, Bart Klem, Stefan van Laar, and Marleen van Klingeren. *Principles and Pragmatism: Civil-Military Action in Afghanistan and Liberia.* Study commissioned by Cordaid, May 2006. <www.cordaid.nl>.

Goodhand, Jonathan. *Aiding Peace: The Role of NGOs in Armed Conflict.* Warwickshire: ITDG Publishing (now Practical Action Publishing), 2006.

Government of Canada. *Canada's International Policy Statement: A Role of Pride and Influence in the World.* Department of Foreign Affairs and International Trade. <http://geo.international.gc.ca/cip-pic/ips/overview-en.aspx>.

Government of Liberia. *Interim Poverty Reduction Strategy Paper,* Dec. 2006. <http://www.imf.org/external/pubs/ft/scr/2007/cr0760.pdf>.

Hancock, Graham. *The Lords of Poverty.* Grove Press/Atlantic Monthly Press; 1st Atlantic Monthly Press Edition, 2000.

International Federation of Red Cross and Red Crescent Societies and the International Committee of the Red Cross. *The Code of Conduct for the International Red Cross and Red Crescent Movement and NGOs in Disaster Relief.* <http://www.icrc.org/Web/Eng/siteeng0.nsf/html/57JMNB#a3>.

International Monetary Fund. *Poverty Reduction Strategy Papers (PRSP),* last updated 6 Oct. 2008. <http://www.imf.org/external/np/prsp/prsp.asp?view=ipr&sort=cty>.

Jett, Dennis C. *Why Peacekeeping Fails.* New York: Palgrave Macmillan, 2001.

Jones, Bruce D. *The Changing Role of the UN in Protracted Crises.* HPG Research Briefing, No. 17: July 2004.

-----. *The UN's Evolving Role in Peace and Security: Background Note.* New York University, Center on International Cooperation. Nov. 2008. <http://www.

cic.nyu.edu/internationalsecurity/docs/The%20UN%20and%20International%20Security%20in%20the%201990s.doc>.

Kumar, Chetan. What Really Works in Preventing and Rebuilding Failed States? *Occasional Paper Series,* Issue 2. Washington, DC: Woodrow Wilson International Centre for Scholars, Dec. 2006.

Leader, Nicholas and Mohammed Haneef Atmar. Political Projects: Reform, Aid, and the State in Afghanistan. In *Nation-Building Unraveled? Aid, Peace and Justice in Afghanistan,* ed. A. Domini, N. Niland, and K. Wermester. Bloomfield, CT: Kumarian Press, 2004.

Lund, M. *What Kind of Peace is Being Built? Assessing the Record of Post-Conflict Peacebuilding, Charting Future Directions.* Ottawa: International Development Research Centre, 2003.

-----. Why This Topic Matters–The Quest for Coherence in Countries at Risk of Conflict. *Comparative Urban Studies Occasional Papers Series,* No. 2. Washington, DC: Woodrow Wilson International Center for Scholars, Dec. 2006.

MacRae, Joanna, ed. *The New Humanitarianisms: A Review of Trends in Global Humanitarian Action.* London, UK: Overseas Development Institute (Humanitarian Policy Group, Report 11), Apr. 2002.

Marin, Michael. *The Road to Hell: The Ravaging Effects of Foreign Aid and International Charity.* New York: Free Press, 2002.

McHugh, Gerard and Lola Gostelow. *Provincial Reconstruction Teams and Humanitarian-Military Relations in Afghanistan.* London, UK: Save the Children, 2004. <http://www.humanitarianinfo.org/darfur/uploads/military/Military%20PRTs%20in%20Afghanistan_Sep04%20by%20SCUK.pdf>.

Milliken, Jennifer, ed. *State Failure, Collapse and Reconstruction.* Oxford: Blackwell, 2003.

Minear, Larry. *The Humanitarian Enterprise: Dilemmas and Discoveries.* Bloomfield, CT: Kumarian Press, 2002.

Moore, Jonathan. Hard Choices: Moral Dilemmas in Humanitarian Intervention. Oxford: Rowman and Littlefield, 1999.

Nan, Susan Allen. *Intervention Coordination. Intractable Conflict Knowledge Base.* Boulder, CO: University of Colorado, Conflict Information Consortium, 2003. <www.beyondintractability.org> [June 2007].

O'Brien, Paul. Old Wood, New Paths, and Diverging Choices for NGOs. In *Nation-Building Unraveled? Aid, Peace and Justice in Afghanistan,* ed. A. Domini, N. Niland, and K. Wermester, 187–206. Bloomfield, CT: Kumarian Press, 2004.

Office for the Coordination of Humanitarian Affairs (OCHA). *Inter-Agency Standing Committee Interim Self-Assessment of the Implementation of the Cluster Approach in the Field.* 15–17 Nov. 2006. <http://ocha.unog.ch/humanitarianreform/Portals/1/cluster%20approach%20page/Introduction/IASC%20Interim%20Self%20Assessment.pdf>.

Olson, Lara. Fighting for Humanitarian Space: NGOS in Afghanistan. *Journal of Military and Strategic Studies* 9, no. 1: Fall 2006. <http://www.jmss.org/2006/2006fall/articles/olson_ngo-afghanistan.pdf>.

Organization for Economic Co-operation and Development. Whole of Government Approaches to Fragile States. *DAC Guidelines and Reference Series:* A DAC Reference Document, 2006.

-----. *Development Assistance Committee Guidelines: Helping Prevent Violent Conflict.* Development Co-operation Directorate (DCD-DAC) 2001. <www.oecd.org/dac/conflict/preventionguidelines>.

-----. *Paris Declaration on Aid Effectiveness.* 2005. <http://www.oecd.org/document/18/0,2340,en_2649_3236398_35401554_1_1_1_1,00.html>.

-----. *Principles for Good International Engagement in Fragile States.* Apr. 2005. <http://www.oecd.org/document/46/0,3343,en_2649_33693550_35233262_1_1_1_1,00.html>.

-----. *Senior Level Forum on Development Effectiveness in Fragile States.* Background papers. 13–14 Jan., 2005. <http://www.oecd.org/document/30/0,3343,en_2649_33693550_33964254_1_1_1_1,00.html>.

-----. *Conflict, Peace and Development Co-operation on the Threshold of the 21st Century, 1997.* <http://www.oecd.org/dataoecd/31/39/2755375.pdf>.

Orr, Robert, ed. Winning the Peace: An American Strategy for Post-Conflict Reconstruction. *CSIS Significant Issues,* No. 26: 2004.

Paris, Roland. *At War's End: Building Peace after Civil Conflict.* Cambridge, UK: Cambridge University Press, 2004.

-----. *Understanding the "Coordination Problem" in Post War State-building.* Research Partnership on Postwar State-building (RPPS). Sustainable Peacebuilding Network (SPN). <http://state-building.org>.

Patrick, Stewart and Kaysie Brown. *Greater than the Sum of Its Parts? Assessing "Whole of Government" Approaches to Fragile States.* New York: International Peace Academy, July 2007.

Peace Operations Monitor. Civilian Monitoring of Complex Peace Operations; Afghanistan. <http://pom.peacebuild.ca/afghanistan.shtml>.

Perito, Robert M. *The U.S. Experience with Provincial Reconstruction Teams in Afghanistan.* Washington, DC: United States Institute of Peace, Oct. 2005. <http://www.usip.org/pubs/specialreports/sr152.html>.

Provincial Reconstruction Teams Executive Steering Committee. Terms of Reference for Combined Force Command and International Security Assistance Force Provincial Reconstruction Teams in Afghanistan. Jan. 2005.

Ricigliano, Robert. Networks of Effective Action: Implementing an Integrated Approach to Peacebuilding. *Security Dialogue,* No. 34, 2003.

Rieff, David. A *Bed for the Night: Humanitarianism in Crisis.* New York: Simon and Schuster, 2002.

Rotberg, Robert I., ed. *When States Fail: Causes and Consequences.* Princeton, NJ: Princeton University Press, 2002.

Rubin, Barnet, Humayun Hamidzada, and Abby Stoddard. *Afghanistan 2005 and Beyond: Prospects for Improved Stability.* Reference Document, Netherlands Institute of International Relations, Clingendael Institute. The Hague:

Royal Government of the Netherlands, Apr. 2005. <http://www.clingendael.nl/publications/2005/20050400_cru_paper_barnett.pdf>.

Shawcross, William. *Deliver Us from Evil: Peacekeepers, Warlords and a World of Endless Conflict.* New York: Simon & Schuster, 2000.

Sida, Lewis. *Challenges to Humanitarian Space: A Review of Humanitarian Issues Related to the UN Integrated Mission in Liberia and to the Relationship Between Humanitarian and Military Actors in Liberia.* Monitoring and Steering Group (MSG), Humanitarian Information Centre for Liberia (HIC Liberia). Apr. 2005. <http://www.humanitarianinfo.org/Liberia/infocentre/general/docs/Challenges%20to%20humanitarian%20space%20in%20Liberia.pdf>.

Smith, Dan. *Towards a Strategic Framework for Peacebuilding: Getting their Act Together.* Overview Report of the Joint Utstein Study of Peacebuilding. Oslo: Royal Norwegian Ministry of Foreign Affairs, Apr. 2004.

Stapleton, Barbara. Presentation on Afghanistan. Copenhagen Seminar on Concerted Planning and Action of Civil and Military Activities in International Operations. 20–21 June 2005. <http://www.acbar.org/downloads/Copenhagen%20Seminar%20(Advocacy).pdf>.

-----. NATO: New Tasks and Responsibilities. Paper presented at the NATO WIIS Conference in Brussells, 11 July 2005. <http://www.acbar.org/downloads/NATO%20(Advocacy).pdf>.

Stedman, Stephen John, Donald Rothchild, and Elizabeth M. Cousens, eds. *Ending Civil Wars: The Implementation of Peace Agreements.* Boulder, CO: Lynne Rienner Publishers, 2002.

Stoddard, Abby and Adele Harmer. *Room to Maneouver: Challenges of Linking Humanitarian Action and Post-Conflict Recovery in the New Global Security Environment.* Occasional Paper, United Nations Development Programme, Human Development Report Office, 2005.

Stoddard, Abby, Adele Harmer, and Katherine Haver. *Providing Aid in Insecure Environments: Trends in Policy and Operations.* Humanitarian Policy Group Report (HPG), 23 Sept. 2006.

Suhrke, Astri. *When More is Less: Aiding State-building in Afghanistan.* Bergen, Norway: Chr. Michelsen Institute (CMI), 2006. <http://www.cmi.no/publications/publication/?2402=when-more-is-less>.

Terry, Fiona. *Condemned to Repeat?: The Paradox of Humanitarian Action.* Ithaca, NY: Cornell University Press, 2002.

Tschirgi, Necla. *Security and Development Policies: Untangling the Relationship.* New York: International Peace Academy, Sept. 2005. <http://www.gsdrc.org/docs/open/CC108.pdf>.

United Nations Development Programme. *Liberia.* <www.lr.undp.org/governances1.htm>.

-----. *Liberia Annual Report, 2005.* <http://www.lr.undp.org/UNDP-LIBERIA_annualreport2005-web.pdf>.

United Nations Development Programme. *National Human Development Report, Liberia.* 2006.

United Nations Office for the Coordination of Humanitarian Affairs (UNOCHA). *Common Humanitarian Action Plan (CHAP).* July 2007. <http://ochaonline.un.org/cap2005/webpage.asp?Page=1546>.

United Nations General Assembly and Security Council. *Report of the Panel on United Nations Peace Operations.* 2000.

United Nations General Assembly Resolution A/RES/60/180, The Peacebuilding Commission. Dec. 2005.

United Nations Peacebuilding Commission. Provisional Guidelines for the Participation of Civil Society in the Meetings of the Peacebuilding Commission, PBC/1/OC/12. June 2007.

United Nations Security Council. Fourteenth Progress Report of the Secretary General on the United Nations Mission in Liberia, S/2007/151.

-----. Comprehensive Review of the Whole Question of Peacekeeping Operations in All Their Aspects, A/55/305 – S/2000/809, Executive Summary, viii. 2000.

-----. Comprehensive Review of the Whole Question of Peacekeeping Operations in All Their Aspects, A/55/305 – S/2000/809, Brahimi Report, 2000.

United Nations Secretary-General's High-level Panel on UN System-wide Coherence in the Areas of Development, Humanitarian Assistance, and the Environment. *Delivering as One.* New York. 9 Nov. 2006.

Welsh, Jennifer M., ed. *Humanitarian Intervention and International Relations.* Oxford: Oxford University Press, 2004.

Williams, Garland H. *Engineering Peace: The Military Role in Post-conflict Reconstruction.* Washington, DC: United States Institute of Peace Press, 2005. <http://www.reliefweb.int/rw/rwb.nsf/db900SID/AMMF-6QDDKH?OpenDocument>.

Woodrow, Peter. *Advancing Practice in Conflict Analysis and Strategy Development.* Cambridge, MA: Collaborative Learning Projects, Reflecting on Peace Practice Project, 2006.

-----. *Theories of Change/Theories of Peacebuilding (draft).* Cambridge, MA: Collaborative Learning Projects, Reflecting on Peace Practice Project Paper, 2006.

World Bank. *Afghanistan. Service Delivery and Governance at the Sub-National Level.* Washington, DC: World Bank, July 2007. Coherence in the Areas of Development, Humanitarian Assistance, and the Environment. *Delivering as One.* New York. 9 Nov. 2006.

Colonel Mike Capstick, OMM, MSM,CD, retired from the Canadian Armed Forces (Regular) in late 2006 after thirty-two years of service. He was the commander of the first deployment of the CF Strategic Advisory Team – Afghanistan from August 2005 until August 2006. This unique unit, a mixed military/civilian team, provided strategic planning advice and capacity building to development related ministries and agencies of the Government of the Islamic Republic of Afghanistan. Currently, he is an associate of the University of Calgary's Centre for Military and Strategic Studies and of the Peacebuilding, Development and Security Programme (a joint endeavour of CMSS and the Institute of World Affairs). mcapstick@shaw.ca

Stephen Cornish has spent more than a decade working with humanitarian organizations including Médecins Sans Frontières and the Canadian Red Cross, and is currently serving as Policy and Advocacy Advisor at CARE Canada. He has been involved in creating humanitarian space and in delivering humanitarian aid in Chechnya, Sierra Leone, Sudan, Rwanda, Colombia, and Haiti, among others. Recently he completed a brief mission to Afghanistan and was able not only to witness the current situation but to compare it to his previous experience of carrying out humanitarian assistance in Afghanistan under the Taliban in 1987. In addition to his field experience, he has an MA in Global Risk and Crisis Management from the Sorbonne in Paris and is completing another MA in Conflict Resolution at the University of Bradford in the United Kingdom. Stephen now lives in Ottawa with his wife, Madina. stevec@care.ca

Cedric de Coning holds a joint research fellow appointment with the Norwegian Institute of International Affairs (NUPI) in Oslo, and the African Center for the Constructive Resolution of Disputes (ACCORD) in Durban, South Africa. He is also contracted to the Civil-Military Coordination Section (CMCS) of the UN's Office for the Coordination of Humanitarian Affairs (OCHA). He worked with the South African Foreign Ministry (1988–97), ACCORD (1997–2000 and 2002–07), the UN Transitional Administration in East Timor (UNTAET) in 1999 and 2001, and the UN Department of Peacekeeping Operations (DPKO) in New York in 2002. Cedric holds an MA (Cum Laude) in Conflict Management and Peace Studies from the University of KwaZulu-Natal and is a D.Phil. candidate at the University of Stellenbosch. cdc@nupi.no

Hrach Gregorian is President of the Institute of World Affairs (IWA), a non-governmental organization specializing in international conflict management and post-conflict peacebuilding. Gregorian co-founded the conflict prevention and resolution organizations. Field experience in Alliance for Peacebuilding (AfP), an international network of applied conflict management and peacebuilding, has taken Gregorian to over twenty countries. He serves on various boards and has faculty appointments in the School of International Service, American University, Washington, D.C.; the Graduate Program in Conflict Management, Royal Roads University, Victoria, Canada; and the Faculty of Social Sciences, University of Calgary, where he co-directs the Peacebuilding, Development, and Security Program housed in the Centre for Military and Strategic Studies. From 1988 to 1994, Gregorian was director of the Education and Training Program at the United States Institute of Peace (USIP). During his tenure there, he also directed the Institute's grant program. Gregorian earned his MA and Ph.D. degrees at Brandeis University. hgregorian@iwa.org

Lara Olson is an associate at the Centre for Military and Strategic Studies and Co-director of the Peacebuilding, Development and Security Program at CMSS. She has extensive experience on practical approaches to improving the effectiveness of NGO humanitarian, development, and peacebuilding efforts in conflict areas. Since the mid-1990s, she has worked as an aid practitioner and with innovative international action-research projects to improve aid outcomes in areas of conflict, including directing the research phase of the ongoing Reflecting on Peace Practice Project from 1999–2003 and conducting training and research on conflict-sensitive approaches. Fluent in Russian, she has worked in the former Soviet Union with field-based NGOs on humanitarian, development, and peacebuilding programming in areas of armed conflict in the Caucasus and in Central Asia. lolson@ucalgary.ca

Barbara J. Stapleton studied Middle East history and politics at the School of Oriental and African Studies at London University and completed her LLM in the international law of human rights at the University of Essex in 1991. She spent the 1980s working in Eritrea, Iranian Kurdistan, Pakistan, Burma, and the Thai-Cambodian border. From 1992–97, she was a consultant to the BBC series *Human Rights, Human Wrongs*. She moved to Afghanistan in October 2002, joining ACBAR, the main NGO coordination body based in Kabul, as Advocacy and Policy Coordinator. In May 2006, she joined the Office of the Special Representative of the EU for Afghanistan in Kabul as a senior political adviser, and is now Deputy to that office. bj.stapleton@yahoo.co.uk